Rookie
Reader

LIGHTNING LIZ

by Larry Dane Brimner

illustrated by Brian Floca

Children's Press®
A Division of Scholastic Inc.
New York • Toronto • London • Auckland • Sydney
Mexico City • New Delhi • Hong Kong
Danbury, Connecticut

For E. Russell Primm III
—L. D. B.

Again, for Elizabeth (of course!)
—B. F.

Reading Consultant
Linda Cornwell
Learning Resource Consultant
Indiana Department of Education

Library of Congress Cataloging-in-Publication Data
Brimner, Larry Dane.
Lightning Liz / by Larry Dane Brimner ; illustrated by Brian Floca.
p. cm. — (A rookie reader)
Summary: An energetic young girl rushes on the way to bake a cake.
ISBN 0-516-20753-9
[1. Speed—Fiction.] I. Floca, Brian, ill. II. Title. III. Series.
PZ7.B767Li 1998
sq] —dc21
                                97-13835
                                    CIP
                                    AC

© 1998 by Larry Dane Brimner
Illustration © 1998 by Brian Floca

Liz is a flash of lightning.

No matter where she goes.
No matter how.

Liz goes in a hurry.

Through the park.

By the school.

On her skates.

On her scooter.

Uphill.

Downhill.

Frontwards . . .

. . . and backwards.

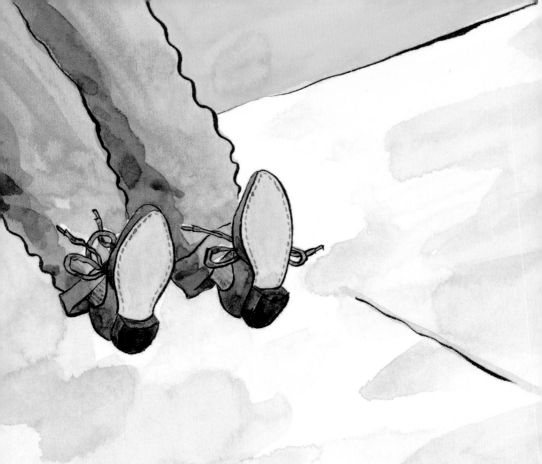

Liz races.

And speeds.

And dashes and darts.

Here and there.
Everywhere.

What would you call
this flash of lightning?

Lightning Liz, of course!

Word List (40 words)

a	flash	Liz	skates
and	frontwards	matter	speeds
backwards	goes	no	the
by	her	of	there
call	here	on	this
course	how	park	through
darts	hurry	races	what
dashes	in	school	where
downhill	is	scooter	would
everywhere	lightning	she	you

About the Author

Larry Dane Brimner writes on a wide range of topics, from picture book and middle-grade fiction to young adult nonfiction. His previous Rookie Readers are *Brave Mary, How Many Ants?,* and *Firehouse Sal.* Mr. Brimner is also the author of *E-mail* and *The World Wide Web* for Children's Press and the award-winning *Merry Christmas, Old Armadillo* (Boyds Mills Press). He lives in the southwest region of the United States.

About the Illustrator

Brian Floca is the author and illustrator of *The Frightful Story of Harry Walfish* and the illustrator of several other books, among them *Poppy,* by Avi (winner of the 1996 *Boston Globe-Horn Book Award* for fiction), *Jenius: The Amazing Guinea Pig,* by Dick King-Smith, and *Luck with Potatoes,* by Helen Ketteman (a *Boston Globe* "best of '95" children's book). Brian Floca grew up in Temple, Texas, and currently lives near Boston, Massachusetts.

DRONE
BALONEY

A Novel
By
John Hewitt

PUMP
ISLAND
TALES

Pump Island Tales
Mill Valley, California

For more information, go to the website: pumpisland.com
Or contact the author at: authors@pumpisland.com

Published by
Pump Island Tales
38 Miller Ave, #247
Mill Valley, CA 94941

To contact: authors@pumpisland.com

ISBN-10: 0615913113
ISBN-13: 978-0615913117

Cover design by Margie Drechsel
Book design by ShubinDesign.com
Typeface: Fairfield, Stencil

For
Scott Amour
Who Taught Us All

Acknowledgements

The now defunct La Coppa Coffee enclave in Mill Valley, California, was a fertile arena of ideas and blather. Thanks to the crowd there plus many wise and talented friends including editors Peter Spear and Annette Blanchard, cover designer Margie Drechsel, book designer Jim Shubin, cartographer Ron Jewett, Bill Hewitt, Gustavo Vazquez and the congenial Baja residents I have met during my travels.

"All the federales say
They could have had him any day
They only let him slip away
Out of kindness I suppose"

—Pancho and Lefty
Townes Van Zandt

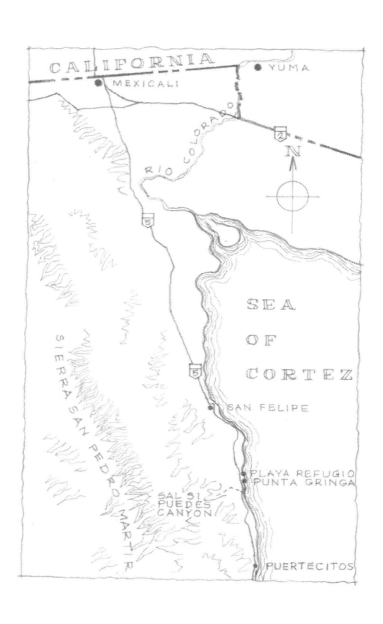

1

Down to Earth

The Sea of Cortez reeked like canned dog food. Blooms of juicy plankton had risen from the depths overnight. Now the blistering sun was slow-roasting the tiny invertebrates as they floated helplessly on the surface. The rotten stench fouled the air along 30-miles of Baja coast below San Felipe.

For the record, the fishing stunk too. Mercury Stiles's 22-foot Whaler, the *Outta Here*, with neighbors Doc and Ruby aboard, had been shutout that morning. Three hours trolling through the nasty odors and there hadn't been even a nibble. The delicious white sea bass—their usual prey—had skittered off to deeper waters. Now a squadron of hungry gulls wheeled and squawked overhead, dive-bombing the Whaler with excrement, upset because their usual share of tasty fish guts was not forthcoming.

Merc was ready to call it a day. He was pulling up the trolling motor when the nearby sea began churning, roiling. An immense creature, shaped like a butterflied shrimp but weighing over a ton, rose through the water 20 feet behind the boat. It breached fully, then rolled over in the air and plunged back in headfirst, waving its signature rattail and sending a torrent of salt water into the skiff.

"What the hell," said Merc, wiping the spray from his face. "That...that was a manta ray." But the enormous undersea beast with 10-foot wingspan wasn't through with the *Outta Here*. It surfaced slowly a second time, eyeballed the Whaler for a minute, swam back to the boat like a dog begging for treats and nudged the stern, as if to apologize.

Ruby leaned over the railing. She found herself face-to-face with a fish whose grapefruit-sized eyeball was attached to a fin protruding from its head. "Our manta ray friend here is the biggest thing I've seen since my ex-husband's ass." She laughed. "But he looks intelligent." And she tentatively reached out and patted the creature's rough skin. "Seems friendly. I read these giant rays have the largest brains of any fish. I wish he could talk so he could tell us what he is doing here."

"Yeah, all we need is a talking giant fish," said Merc. "He's only hungry and here to slurp up the rotting goodies in this vile-smelling red tide." And with that, the manta backed away from the Whaler, playfully rolled its body exposing its white underbelly, raised its wings in a vague piscine salute and then swam off, skipping along the surface and scooping up the available plankton as if they were ambrosia.

"Well, that was bizarre," said Doc. "In person, that is

one spectacular creature. I had heard there was a manta somewhere near here. I hope I never get that close again. If he landed on the Whaler, he would have flattened us."

Doc picked up the binoculars and stretched out again on the *Outta Here's* back seat cushions, contemplating the cloudless sky. "You know, we seem to have another visitor. A silver private plane has been circling us for several minutes. He's still up there."

"It must be lost. We're two miles offshore," said Merc, drying himself off. He finally raised the trolling motor, then started the skiff's outboard and turned to his boat mates. "We're done here. It's back to Punta Gringa."

"Before we go, give the hopeless fish finder one more try," said Doc. "If the little son-of-a-bitch doesn't work this time, throw it over the side."

Merc had traded for the cheesy-looking device last week, getting it from a local merchant for five quarts of synthetic outboard oil. He flipped the finder's toggle power switch to on, but it jammed. He pushed harder with his thumb but ended up snapping the button off the plastic case. There was a bright flash and an electrical crackle, and the acrid odor of burning insulation. Merc took a shock and fell backwards. "Yow."

Then—a popping sound overhead.

Doc still had the binoculars. "Something happened to the plane's engine." The aircraft stopped circling and made a desperate turn toward the coastline. "It's cutting out. What the hell is that all about?" said Doc.

A thin wisp of smoke trailed from the plane. It was rocking back and forth as it headed for the shore.

Merc shifted the *Outta Here* into neutral and stared.

Although the pilot appeared to regain some control, this distressed aircraft was clearly a goner. His gut tightened. *Heaven help the people* inside, he thought. By the time the silver plane reached the coastline south of their trailers on the Punta Gringa sandspit, its sputtering engine had stopped. Silently, the doomed craft began to cartwheel, rolling over and over until it plunged toward the hardpan desert floor, striking the ground with a thunderous crunch that could be heard for miles.

The trio on the Whaler sat stunned. Doc said, "We should try to help."

Merc pointed the bow toward the crash site, shoved the throttle to max and sped landward. Ruby held on tight. Just before they reached shore, he shut the outboard down, signaled Doc to raise the motor and the *Outta Here* skidded through the swells, across a sandbar and up onto the beach.

"All okay?" Merc had grabbed the fire extinguisher.

Everyone made their way through the loose desert sand, carefully avoiding the ankle-puncturing cactus spines. Reaching the wreckage, they could see the aircraft's tail was destroyed but the front fuselage was intact. Still, there would be no crew, no passengers to pull out.

They were standing beside the crumpled remains of a pilotless U.S. government aircraft—a drone.

Doc used the extinguisher to put out the small fire. Everyone could clearly see the markings on the craft's undamaged nosecone—the official seal of the U.S. Customs and Border Protection and a foot high graphic: Charley 3.

Merc had seen pictures of these clandestine spycraft

but had never been this close. What the hell was a U.S. drone doing 150 miles south of the border in Baja? This crumpled intruder was bound to become more than a regrettable accident. A drone crash would attract a flood of military investigators, police and journalists to their sandspit where the suspicious residents cherished isolation before everything else. He feared his idyllic life was headed for the outhouse.

Within minutes of the crash, an unmarked Mexican military helicopter clattered in and offloaded soldiers with body armor and automatic weapons. Well-disciplined, they formed a ring around the downed bird, discouraging the curious onlookers from scavenging debris. Shortly after that, U.S. military personnel landed in a second chopper and surrounded Merc, Doc and Ruby. Unsmiling, they held them at gunpoint.

A much more congenial officer in a camouflage U.S. uniform finally appeared and ordered the guards to back off. "Sorry about the weapons. Where exactly are we and what is that smell?"

"Just south of Punta Gringa. About 30 miles below San Felipe. And the smell is a red tide. Mostly rotting plankton," said Merc

"Thank you for putting out the fire. We need to interview each of you about what you saw as the aircraft approached the land."

Merc, Doc and Ruby had finished giving accounts when a third chopper roared in, then hovered arrogantly for minutes while its rotor down wash blew stinging sand into everyone's eyes. This time Agent Tank Dolan of U.S Customs and Border Protection and two assistants jumped out. Tank was in charge and he was seething, desperately looking for someone to blame in the crash of his four-million-dollar drone. The affable officer who had done the earlier interviews briefed Dolan on the three Punta Gringans first to the crash site.

Dolan tucked in his pressed uniform shirt and walked brusquely up to the trio. He sneered as if they had just been caught red-handed with a boatload of baby seal pelts and heroin. His attitude was confrontational. "I am Agent Dolan with the Department of Homeland Security and I want to know how you got to the crash scene so fast?"

"We were just offshore fishing," said Ruby.

Dolan consulted his notes. "Who is Will Tedford, the former Air Force flight surgeon?"

"That's me," said Doc, wearing shabby swim trunks and an unbuttoned Hawaiian shirt featuring psychedelic fish and brown-skinned women. A chain around his neck held his old military ids.

"And I see you still have your dog tags."

Doc nodded. "Memories."

"Being air force, I assume you know a lot about drones," said Dolan.

"Being air force, I worked in the hospital in Germany. But I also don't know shit about drones."

Dolan didn't smile. "Let me be straight with all three of you. We had your boat under surveillance. We saw one of you reaching out of the boat, possibly passing drugs or something to an undersea contact. We saw a muzzle flash by the helm console, and then detected an electronic signal just before our engine shut down. I want to inform you that you might be suspects in the crash of this drone. Where is your boat now?"

Doc bristled. "You were watching us? Then you know we were out fishing. And yes one of us patted a visiting manta ray. And our fish finder fried itself. Then we rushed ashore to put out the sparky little fire on your piece of shit drone."

"That's not what we saw."

"Maybe you only saw what you wanted to see. Maybe you've got an agenda and you don't really care what goes on down on the ground." Doc pointed to the Whaler, beached on the shoreline. "Merc's boat is right over there."

Dolan signaled to the two assistants in jump suits standing nearby. They wore blue latex gloves and paper masks over their mouths and noses. "First, hand over that fire extinguisher to my men. Then, we'll just check out the so-called fishing boat."

Everyone surrounded Merc's skiff. It was ten feet from the water. Dolan brushed off his polished street shoes and climbed inside. He opened a few lockers beneath the seats. "Fishing? Where's the fish?"

"Didn't catch any this morning," said Merc.

"So, the three of you usually go out and don't catch anything?"

"There was a bad red tide today. Foul plankton."

Dolan ordered his men to remove the three fishing rods, a bait bucket, a toolbox with lures, eight empty beer bottles, and the small cooler and place everything on the sand. They detached the half-destroyed fish-finder, still smoking in its imitation leather case, from the helm console and handed it to Dolan. "This looks like a GPS guidance device," he said.

"I wish it were. It's a worthless piece of crap fish finder," said Merc.

"And where did you buy it?"

"I traded to the Acosta brothers for it."

"Do you have a receipt for it?"

"You don't get receipts down here. It's Mexico."

Dolan handed it to his lackeys who unscrewed the back, looked inside, and placed the pieces in a blue plastic bag. The heat and stink were getting to the hatless Dolan. He continually shaded his eyes against the intense sun. Sweat stains on his deep green shirt reached from his armpits to his waist. He jumped back out of the Whaler. "Check out everything else in this boat. Look for hidden electronics. Check out the forward anchor locker and bait well." He paused for effect. "I just don't understand going out fishing and not catching anything, not even a little fish."

"Get hosed," said Doc. Dolan ignored him.

The assistants began disassembling the beer cooler. They stripped out the lining and snapped the bottom in half. It turned out to be nothing more than pebbly insulating foam. Clearly frustrated, Dolan booted the cooler into the nearby mesquite bushes.

Merc was irritated. "I hope you guys pay me for the cooler. They don't grow on trees, you know."

"Shut up. You're lucky you're not in chains." Dolan waited two minutes while the assistants made another pass at the boat. They found nothing in the *Outta Here*.

One made a thumbs down gesture.

"You guys live around here?"

"Just down the beach."

"I don't know how you can stand the smell. This place stinks like all of Mexico."

"It only stinks when coarse bastards like you fly in," said Doc.

"I'll run more tests on your so-called fish finder. It had better not be some sort of telemetry device. Otherwise, I guess you can leave. Don't take your boat. I want my men to give it another once over. We'll be in touch."

"Hey. I'd rather take my boat. If we don't get back in the water soon, the tide will be out and then it'll be stranded," said Merc.

"When we are done here, come get it. If your boat is stranded, then wait until tomorrow when the tide is back in. Oh, and one other thing, don't talk to anyone about this crash."

"Why the fuck not? Who are you to tell me who I can and cannot talk to?" said Doc.

"Take it easy, doctor. You are former air force. Be patriotic. This is a matter of national security."

Merc had never seen Doc so incensed. "Whose national security? This is Mexico, in case you haven't noticed. We're 150 miles into Mexico. Mexico. It's not the U.S."

Dolan steamed. "I'm agent Tank Dolan from the Customs and Border Protection. Watch your mouth. If you know what is good for you, don't say anything."

Doc was edging closer to Dolan. "I'll say whatever I want. I spent six years in the frigging air force, saving lives.

When I left, they cheap ass screwed me out my medical benefits and the health care for my partner. That's why I'm living in a trailer on a beach in Mexico. You can take your air force and shove it, agent stick it up your ass."

Since his military days, Doc had ballooned a bit and now outweighed the trimmer Dolan by at least one hundred pounds. He had edged up to within a foot from the border agent's face.

Dolan could smell the beers Doc had polished off while fishing. He reached down and unsnapped the safety strap atop the Beretta pistol in its belt holster. On the flight down, he had pulled the slider and put a round in the chamber. If Doc came at him, he would defend himself with deadly force.

Merc grabbed Doc and wrestled him away, taking him to the ground. Dolan walked to where they sprawled in the dirt.

"Tedford. Or Doc. I don't like you and I can make your life hell. I know you've got something to do with this."

Merc and Doc stood up and brushed off the sand. The latex-gloved assistants were taking the cover off the outboard when Ruby finally picked up the fishing poles, the bait, and the broken cooler. "We'd better get out of here."

The three began to walk along the shore back to the Punta Gringa sandspit. Doc frothed. "I don't understand these stupid fucks jacking us around. We save their lame frigging drone from getting burned up in a fire and this small-brained hard ass grills us. And why? Because I was in the air force? That makes a lot of sense. I've had a bellyful of this bullshit. How in the hell does that make us suspicious?"

Merc was worried. "Look. I know you've got a hard on for the air force. But you've got to play it cool. That idiot was going for his sidearm. If he wants to, he can cause us all sorts of grief."

"Oh. Stop being such a pussy, Merc. Sometimes you have to get in people's faces."

"And sometimes that backfires. Still, it is strange, isn't it?" said Merc. "We thought it was a tourist plane. Instead, it was the government eyeballing us. I fear we are going to see more of these guys."

—∞—

Two hours later, as an interested sandspit crowd watched from Doc's patio, a heavy-lift Sea Knight tandem rotor chopper wobbled in from the north. The crew hustled the U.S. troops aboard, hooked Charley 3's wreckage to a sling and the helicopter whisked it away. That was it. The remaining Mexican federal troops cleansed the crash site and raked the surface until the previously worthless desert land again looked worthless. Then they left by truck. An hour after that, Merc and Doc returned, pushed the boat back into the water, started the outboard and piloted it north, covering the half-mile back to the sandspit.

Despite a major effort to cover it up, the story leaked out. A four-million-dollar Homeland Security drone nicknamed Charley 3, based in Yuma, Arizona, under the command of Agent Tank Dolan, had death-spiraled into the desert 150 miles south of the border, near the fishing village of Playa Refugio. The Customs and Border

Protection spokespeople reported the cause was simple—
that the engine quit when it ran out of gas.

But the news jackals sniffed and didn't buy that PR
line. "Charley 3 is Brought Down." "Charley's Angels Sink
to Earth." "Drone the Victim of the Cartel." The newspaper stories headlined a continuing battle between the
local drug cartel known as Equipo 30 and the secretive
joint anti-smuggling operation of Mexican and U.S. agencies. The articles noted the cartel's Facebook threats to
attack the Predators, the drones they called los moscos—
the mosquitoes.

For a brief time, television trucks and news reporters
did flood the insular Punta Gringa beach camp. The
locals resolutely ignored reporters' questions and refused
to talk. No one broke the pact. The Punta Gringans threw
eggs and rocks at photographers. They stuffed dead seag-
ull carcasses into their news vans' microwave dishes.

The stonewalling worked. The journalists, getting no
results, balanced the value of any new scraps of information against the ordeal of spending more time in a rathole
encampment where the outhouses were moved only once
a year. And so they left.

Merc was troubled. He knew in his heart that something primal had changed. For the recluses like himself
hiding out in the tumbledown beach settlements up and
down the coast, the drone falling from the sky was a mete-
or exploding in their midst.

2

Pings From Above

Border Protection pilot Enrique Castillo leaned forward in his comfortable leather chair. His body was in an air-conditioned trailer at the Yuma, Arizona airport but his mind was 180-miles deep into Mexico, where he was piloting the surveillance drone Charley 2 towards a good-sized yacht anchored offshore Puertecitos on the east Baja coast.

His mission was to identify drug runners, but he couldn't pass up an opportunity for a quick interlude. Castillo locked the hi-resolution spy scope on a sunbather in the skimpy swimsuit on the yacht's foredeck. She was hot. His lens lingered at her glossy red toenails, and then drifted lazily across her back and up to her bare shoulders. Now the clock was ticking. How long could he gawk before the Captain caught him?

Gotta be smart, Enrique.

Castillo was a trainee drone pilot with a palpable weakness—duly noted numerous times in his agency personnel dossier—that he took pains to fly low and aim the powerful cameras at any bikini or skinny-dipper he could find.

He punched in a code labeling the lounging woman "suspect 1". Regulations required a closer look.

The magnification was cranked as far as it would go. Now he could focus on the sweat puddle in the small of her back.

And could count the lettuce leaves in the chicken salad on her towel.

And read the model number on the piece lying next to her salad—a Glock 21 semi-automatic handgun. Ouch.

His mystery woman sensed leering from above. She fidgeted, and gazed skyward.

Bingo. There, on Castillo's full screen monitor, a very familiar face with a broken nose and scar high on her cheek. *Oh Mama. It's Iris Lopez again. You're very sweet brown sugar but we've busted you before. Baby, you are the give-away this morning.*

Forbidden dawdling had indeed paid off. Iris was a notorious drug cartel scout, so Enrique was off the hook. He shifted his attention to the stern of the craft anchored a quarter mile from the beach. Back there, the boat's crew joked and goofed around while they loaded suspicious blue plastic containers onto a skiff that had pulled alongside. He could read the drug manufacturer's company name "Zabell S.A." on the barrels.

Toast. You guys are toastola.

Enrique's smirk widened. He radioed an alert to the *federales*—the Mexican federal police. A ground-based pursuit team was only ten minutes away. While Castillo continued to circle above the yacht, the federales roared down a dirt road to confront the criminals unloading the open panga onto the beach. A Mexican coastal patrol boat later seized the larger vessel.

The day's catch: a quarter-million dollar boat, six low-level suspects, Iris Lopez for the sixty-sixth zillionth time and a dozen twenty-gallon containers of pseudoephedrine tablets bound for a meth lab hidden back in the hills. Score? One for the agents—nil for a local drug cartel.

For pilot agent Castillo, these high tech eye-in-the-sky operations were a hell of a lot more comfortable than the eighteen gritty months he spent as a probationary border agent-in-training, rattling around rutted desert roads in four-wheel drive Suburbans, running after suspects who bolted out into the sandy landscape, often tackling them into disgusting cactus patches, or even taking a punch or two in the face. Now he left the sweat, the discomfort, the bruising and the dangerous arrests to others.

Charley 2 was nearly 200 miles south of the border, as deep into Mexico as he could fly. Castillo pumped the aircraft's rudder pedals and uttered a loud "Wooeee" before making a sweeping turn back toward Arizona. Piloting these birds excited him.

He would follow the coastline home, a path that would take him above a border agent's nightmare—the haphazard collection of ancient trailers, one-room hideaways and isolated squatter camps, hideouts with names like Annie's Ranch or Punta Gringa, settlements that snaked up 60 miles of beachfront. Any one could harbor a homecooker meth lab.

Years ago, the U.S. government had given the Customs and Border Protection Agency four surplus Predator drones. These pilotless aircraft were worn out— older models, unarmed warbirds left over from the Middle East. Each had been upgraded with the latest spy lenses and synthetic aperture radar for seeing through haze and smoke.

The Yuma staff had unimaginatively but affectionately nicknamed the drones Charley 1, 2, 3, and 4. Only two were flyable. Charley 3 had crashed last week. Charley 4 was a dog—out of service and being cannibalized for parts. Only Charleys 1 and 2 were mission ready.

Castillo was on the home stretch, kicking back and unwrapping his pungent double bacon GrandeBurger, when the first buzzer screeched. Then more whistles and blinking dials. The mid-air collision-warning alert flashed red. His console lit up like a cheap slot machine. A synthesized woman's voice shrieked "Nose down. Nose down." In the monitor, he could see the drone's forward camera shake as if hit by a hammer. He almost choked on a French fry.

What the deuce was going on?

Enrique jumped on the intercom. "Captain Dolan. Captain. Quick."

His supervisor, air interdiction agent Tank Dolan, required that his underlings address him as Captain, his former rank in the air force where they had real pilots. He was in the trailer next door, busy with a crossword puzzle. Dolan sighed, put down the paper and walked over. "What is it, Castillo?"

"Captain. A thump. Weird. Like last week. It set off

the collision alarm voice warning. It's crazy...something bumped Charley 2 again. Bumped it on the top."

Dolan frowned when he smelled the burger and fries that Castillo had shoved into the wastebasket. Food was off limits in the flight control trailers.

"Hey, first. Congrats on the bust today. Watched it on the monitor. But you spent way too much time giving that swimsuit the once-over."

"Captain. Regs required me to check if she was armed."

"Right, Castillo. You still spent a lot of time checking her out. You were goddam lucky it turned out to be Iris and she had a piece."

"Captain. Here's today's bump. Watch Charley 2 shudder." Castillo toggled the joystick.

Dolan considered the replay. He only saw a slight vibration in the monitor. "Not sure what that was, Castillo. Maybe just turbulence. I don't know."

They both checked the console's gauges. Nothing out of the ordinary. The trusty Predator drone was humming contentedly at ninety miles an hour, its Rotax engine cranking along. It was still over two miles up and locked onto its GPS source. There was no hint of any ground-based radar tracking him. Maybe, mused the Captain, a hatch door had come loose, something that buffeted in the wind stream and fell off the Predator.

"Captain, there was a bump...and it had to come from above."

"Relax, Enrique. If anyone wanted to bring Charley 2 down, they would come at us from below. Isn't that right, Castillo? From bee-low," he said, dragging out the word. "So I don't understand this bullshit about unknown forces thumping our birds on the top."

Enrique was tenacious. "Captain, but that's why this is so bizarre. Somebody or something is banging on the drone from above."

"Well, that little shake doesn't sell me."

"Captain, you should take a second look."

"Castillo. Goddamit. Get the sci-fi cobwebs out of your brain. You are suggesting we've got visitors from some outer space air force—aliens—and I just don't buy it." Dolan kicked the wastebasket in frustration. "Look Enrique. I'm still trying to explain to my boss how we lost Charley 3. I don't need any more grief."

"Captain. We need to pay attention. This might be more of the same."

Dolan appeared to give up. "Well, have maintenance check Charley 2 when he's back in the barn. Bring me the results in the morning."

Castillo sent an on-line text to the ground crew to be ready for an inspection when the craft returned, then retrieved his burger from the trash.

—✼—

The foothills that guard the Mexican coastline along the Sea of Cortez are barren, stark and imposing. There is not a crumb of vegetation—the landscape looks like it has been seared by a giant blowtorch. The rarely visited steep-sided canyons and rocky washes create inhospitable landscapes. West of Playa Refugio, one particularly twisted maze branches out in four directions from a single sandy riverbed. This junction is the gateway to an area so foreboding that it is called Sal Si Puedes, or Get Out If You Can.

On the hillside back in these dry arroyos, miles from the seacoast, a solitary figure stepped inside a hidden cave and whooped for joy. His celebration included popping open a lukewarm Pacifico beer. He was wearing a pair of shorts, flip-flops and a tee-shirt with a handwritten inscription "The H-Man,"

He had shortened his name to H. That would do. Simplicity was important. H worked alone. His home-made drone interceptor, which he nicknamed the Courtesan and which was only one-quarter the Predator's size, today had flown to a position directly above the Border Protection drone's blind spot in front of its tail-mounted pusher propeller. Relying on infrared sensors, his Courtesan snuggled closer to the Predator before launching a miniature flying wing called a Remora, designed to stick a three-inch wide metal disk to the Predator's fuselage. Once attached, the disk's transmitter circuits planted a virus in the larger drone's on-board guidance program. This would open a backdoor portal to later visits from the Remoras.

When its dirty work was done, the Remora and its disk slipped off and fell away to the desert below. The Courtesan mothership, its intimate needs satisfied for now, rose up, veered to the right, and used internal navigation to head for a landing near H's hidden retreat.

H had been shadowing Yuma's anti-drug drones for a month, intercepting Charley 2's telemetry data to decode the Predator's patrol patterns. The encrypted packets revealed a lot—the drone's designation Charley 2 and the pilot's name—Enrique Castillo.

Reprisals should be coming. The U.S. government boys didn't like anyone messing with their drones. H had been there, in those Predator trailers, and he could guess where the officials might take it. The air force was loaded with weapons—decoy drones, high performance Reaper bodyguard drones with Hellfire missiles, field agents who came to the desert banging on doors, or sinister undercover snoops. Trusting anyone was now out of the question.

H knew miscalculations could be devastating. What if this agent Enrique Castillo and his drone pilot buddies were as smart as he was? Or smarter? No. He doubted that. That would never happen.

"They'll find out whom they are up against," H said to no one in particular. "I'll bag one of theirs. Nobody treats me like crap. They owe me that Predator."

H dragged his beat-up plastic patio chair out to the cave's entrance and settled into the shade beneath his homebuilt thatched palm awning. This tiny open space was hidden behind rock formations jutting from the exposed strata. He worked outside until just before dark, when he climbed down to a nearby canyon floor to retrieve the Courtesan. After it was buttoned up and hidden, he camouflaged the cavern opening and headed back to civilization for supplies.

TO SAN FELIPE

N

SAN MARCOS
AIRSTRIP

PLAYA
REFUGIO

PUNTA
GRINGA

BATTERY
PLANT

SANDSPIT

3

La Gringa

The Governor yawned, dealt five cards and announced this was the last hand. Beer bottles and crumbs littered the green velvet poker table. Most of the players had gone home. But Padre Ignacio Belem, the populist Catholic priest known to everyone as Macho Nacho, was fired up. "This one for La Gringa?" he asked.

The Governor nodded. "Claro."

The Padre inspected his cards, called for one from the deck, and smiled.

The Governor took one card himself, said "Chingado" and then threw his hand on the table in disgust.

The Padre laid down a full house, aces high. And with that, a winning poker hand had settled another fishy Baja political deal. The next afternoon, when the Governor signed the papers, the rocky canyon, hot springs, cliff and sandspit 30 miles south of San Felipe was rechristened Punta La Gringa.

Padre Nacho remained blasé about his card table

coup. "True," he acknowledged, "I am a priest for the church. And the name La Gringa? Yes, it's to honor a woman who is a shaman—a mystic. And yes, the governor had resisted, saying the state of Baja California Norte should not recognize witchcraft, and should not name the spot after a foreigner. But I simply pointed out what happened. The Miracle. The heroics and all. Saving the fishermen. It was charismatic. The old name, Punta Chale, meant nothing. La Gringa is a hero to me—and to his people. Tourists will be enthralled by the story of the brave fishermen. And, in the end, God must have agreed. That's why He gave me the aces."

Years ago, Padre Macho Nacho had taken over the 200-mile long parish territory that stretched from the international border south to Puertecitos. Soon he was on road daily, blasting ranchero music from his ratty pickup. The idealistic young priest turned up everywhere, battling for the rights of poor villagers, bringing medical care to remote ranchitos, picking fights with exploiting employers or filling the role as a social worker, family counselor, job-finding agency and compassionate listener for his flock.

In return, the voiceless adored their saintly padre who had never taken a peso for his nonstop commitment to the poor, who often slept in his truck and who lived off the gift meals and cold beer they provided. So when they heard Punta Chale would get new name and that it was Padre Nacho's idea, they backed it. If the Padre thought a more modern name was a good idea—fine with them.

Stuffy conservative church factions were not pleased. Naming a chunk of Mexican coastline after a foreign sorceress was wrong. They took the low road, spreading tawdry gossip about the Padre's controversial movements, questioning his overnight pilgrimages to the goat farm of the sorceress La Gringa. But his supporters rallied behind him. "So what," the villagers said. "That's his business. The padre is probably digging deeper into her herbal remedies. Besides, he has to park his truck somewhere."

The padre was a devout supporter of any scheme to boost the tourist count in Baja. Changing the name of a long-ignored coastal arroyo south of the fishing village of Playa Refugio to La Gringa was part of his plan. But to make it work he needed publicity. So, some say, he urged a local photographer to stage the now famous photos of half-naked campers frolicking in the canyon's hot-water springs, knowing the glossy travel magazines would pick those up. Also, he let slip the canyon's reputation as the chosen home base of mysterious La Gringa, the sorceress and practitioner of the dark arts who used visions and hallucinations while treating ailments.

La Gringa didn't need any pastoral flackery. She was no lightweight mystic. Her potions for cactus spines, scorpion bites, depression or melancholy had become famous. Important politicians, delegados, judges, celebrated matadors, police captains, drug agents, and movie stars joined the throngs making the trip to her goat farm for cleansing sessions. Locals swore on their mother's grave that she appeared in visions. Others repeated stories about mysterious encounters with her on the road.

Even the local fishermen, the *pangueros* who ventured out into the dangerous tidal currents in open skiffs called pangas, idolized her for the *Milagro*—the miracle.

The Milagro is duly recorded in the Baja California Norte's archives. It began when the incompetent captain of a fishing schooner heading south along the coast hired ten pangueros from Playa Refugio to crew for him on a two-day hunt for barracuda. Conditions were dangerous —a moonless night with choppy seas and shrieking wind. A tremendous tidal bore wave pushing north toward the Rio Colorado slammed broadside into their boat, capsizing it and tossing all souls into the warm shark-infested waters.

The next day, the captain's body washed up in the shorebreak at Playa Refugio. The shocked villagers took to the sea in a frantic hunt for survivors. Within hours one panga had reached Punta Chale and the rescuers found all the hired pangueros dazed, shivering, hungry but alive. They jabbered about a woman standing on the shoreline cliff—and how she tended a signal fire, pointing the way to safety between the dangerous rocks. But when they reached the beach, they found no ashes from the bonfire or no sign of the siren. Instead, there were only bundles of goat cheese and a curious aroma of oranges. The woman had disappeared. It had to have been La Gringa.

Padre Nacho's plan for a Punta Gringa tourist mecca backfired. Instead of paying visitors, the isolated sandspit became a haven for penniless loners, shiftless wanderers, fugitives, dropouts and strays that set up a crude beachside trailer camp. Those who moved in lived by the community's motto—"live in what you want, however you want, but help your neighbor while minding your own frigging business." This insular tranquility lasted a decade and the sandspit's reputation grew.

Mercury Stiles heard about La Gringa from a former lover. Four years ago, fleeing from ex-wives and personal threats, he had driven his old Chevy pickup south across the border. Two miles outside Playa Refugio, he slowed to avoid a herd of goats in the road. As he waited for the animals to clear a path, an overpowering fragrance of newly cut citrus flooded the truck's cab and the thin face of a woman with deep brown skin and a wild shock of chestnut hair appeared at the truck's window. The shepherdess gazed at him with piercing grey eyes, reached out and touched his hand, smiled and pointed down a slight grade. She said "Punta Gringa. Bienvenidos," and then vanished along a dirt trail.

What the hell? Merc got out and stood on the overlook. Before him stretched a beach filled with shacks and old trailers scattered helter-skelter amid the mesquite bushes and junked pickups. It was so run-down that Merc liked it immediately. He coasted down and parked, drank a beer, and stretched out to sleep in the pickup's cab.

When the sun rose, his truck was an oven. He wandered out in the sticky morning heat among the shelters and decrepit trailers. There appeared to be no store, no telephones, no electric lines or no order to this tumble-down community.

Beside an old aluminum trailer, a gaunt man with a bushy beard and long gray hair pulled into a ponytail was swearing under the hood of an ancient pickup.

"Those are great old trucks, the '76 F-150s," said Merc.

The man he would come to know as RJ looked up and eyed Merc with a mistrustful gaze. "Jesus loves you," he said. "And, uh, who are you?"

"I'm Mercury Stiles." Merc held out his hand but the man ignored it.

"That's a strange name. Mercury?"

"It's really Mercury Evinrude. My father repaired outboard motors. He named me after his favorite engine."

"What do you want, Mercury?"

"Looking for a place to kick back a few months."

"Don't know of any."

"I'm also looking for someone named RJ."

The Reverend J. Cristo looked up deadpan. "Don't know anyone named RJ."

"Look. His sister Sandra said he lived on this sand-spit. I hooked up with her in L.A. She said her brother James was a former minister and had landed in Punta Gringa, calling himself RJ. Maybe he uses some other name too."

The man under the hood looked up again but said nothing.

"Look. Sandra has a scorpion tattooed under her right shoulder blade."

"Red or green?" asked RJ.

"Actually, it was kind of yellow, and is right next to a flaming skull." Merc was convinced this would open the door. He stuck out his hand again.

The mechanic didn't smile, didn't shake his hand but continued working on the engine.

Merc pulled his hand back. "I need a place for a couple of months."

RJ pointed to a dusty 1949 Streamlite trailer, up on blocks with the exterior aluminum cladding partially torn off. A half-collapsed wooden deck surrounded it. "Don't know why, but if you are interested in staying in an oven like that, you should understand that the heat this morning is just a sample. It will get hotter than the lower circles of hell in the next months. Live in Punta Gringa and you haul your own water, dig your own outhouse, and exist without electricity. You will hate it."

"I can live with that."

"Then go back north two miles to Playa Refugio and make a deal with the scorpion lady. If you are a drug agent or cop, forget it. She'll eat you alive. Be street smart or religious and you'll do okay." RJ affixed a torque wrench to an engine bolt and gave it a twist. "Do you believe in God, Mister Mercury Stiles?"

This came out of left field. Did he want to argue about Merc's vague beliefs? Should Merc reveal his distaste for organized religion? "I do, but not in the way most people do."

"Well, I suggest you dust off your religiosity, brother. When you talk with the scorpion lady, you'll understand."

Merc was baffled. "Not sure I understand."

RJ wiped the oil off his hands. "Well, it's simple. That woman who rents out these places thinks she is god."

"What's her name?"

"Cortez. Gabriela Cortez. She's the boss. Her communal ejido group owns all this land, this very sandspit. And a number of the businesses in the village. And the politicians in San Felipe. She's smart and doesn't suffer fools. She's a force of nature...and she's a bitch, if you'll excuse the expression. She'll size you up. If you two don't click, not only will you never rent in Punta Gringa, you probably don't have a chance in hell of finding anything south of San Felipe. She's honest but I've never seen her smile. Not once."

"She's that tough and she's in charge?"

"Oh yeah." RJ cocked his head. "You'd better believe it."

"So," and Merc held out his hand one more time, "who shall I tell her I talked to?"

RJ still made no move to shake the proffered palm. "Just tell her you talked to one of her ratas—the rats—on the sandspit."

Merc headed back into Playa Refugio, uneasy about meeting this Maria Gabriela Cortez. She was not hard to find. Her desk in the ejido office was behind a floor to ceiling window on the only street in the two-block long village. From where she sat, she kept an eye on everything. Señora Gaby was busy pushing paper.

Merc stood outside, sensing he needed a shower. His tee-shirt reeked of dried sweat. He even detected an aura of oranges that lingered from his brief encounter the night before.

Maybe his half-assed command of Spanish would help.

His entrance was tentative. Gabriela barely looked up. When he asked to rent, she made him stand in the middle of the room until she rose from her chair. Merc was surprised at how tiny she was—easily a foot shorter than him and she couldn't have weighed more than a hundred pounds. Her bushy dark hair was pulled straight back through the back of a black baseball cap. A pair of dark glasses with thick silver frames sat atop the hat. Her blue jeans, running shoes, and cotton polo shirt looked fresh and crisp. A no-nonsense style—efficient, businesslike.

Gaby circled Merc without saying a word. *Here's a new one*, she thought. *Lean, possibly fifty, gray goatee and short, amateurishly trimmed hair with a stubby ponytail in the back. Probably did it himself. Craggy face and good teeth. Nice smile. A bit smelly. Black tee-shirt, jeans, and work boots. Looks as if he has street smarts. Doesn't appear destitute. Definitely not a drug agent or member of the cartel.*

"What attracted you to our sandspit at Punta Gringa, Senor Stiles?"

"It's peaceful. I'm a desert rat at heart. And this exotic goat shepherd pointed it out."

Gaby picked up on the faint orange aroma. This man was carrying the residual citrus fragrance that sticks to people who have encountered La Gringa. She began to feel dizzy, unsteady.

She moved closer. Their faces were only a foot apart. The whiff of citrus now overwhelmed. She looked Merc in the eye. "Hijole—wow. The oranges. Tell me. What did she do in the vision?"

"It wasn't a vision. She was there beside my rear view mirror. She reached in and touched my hand. She waved and pointed and said "Punta Gringa. Bienvenidos.""

Gaby wanted desperately to touch the same spot but held back. "You are indeed blessed, my friend. You have encountered La Gringa. She has come to you. This powerful woman with the strange grey eyes is a curandera, a mystic practitioner of the healing arts. Her potions will cure your scorpion stings or jellyfish welts. Meeting her was an omen to bless the rest of your stay with us."

Satisfied, she sat back down, took Merc's money, wrote out a receipt and rented him the parcel with the rusted out trailer next to RJ's place. "Be patient. It will take you months, even years to be accepted by those suspicious pendejos—the ratas who live on the sandspit," she said.

But Gaby was still edgy. This meeting was not over. She looked down at her hand. It trembled. It had been an achingly long time. Why had this particular gringo put her off her act? Why had he, of all people, been chosen by magical fates to cross paths with La Gringa?

It was a conversation spiraling into weirdness. "I had a vision of her last week," said Gaby, "and La Gringa commanded me to ask a particular question. She didn't say who would answer, but I think it is you."

Merc was tense. Gaby blurted out "This is that question—Do you dance, Senor Mercury Stiles?"

Too strange. Baffled, Merc could only remember the words from an old song. "Well I do, but when I do, it's like the devil possesses me." He grinned.

She smiled back. "That is the right answer. And someday we'll have to see about that."

That was it. She caught herself. Turning her back to him, she resumed her role as Gabriela the all-powerful ejido boss and said, "*Bienvenidos*—welcome—to Mexico." Without another word, she was back to work.

4

Naughty Narco Queen

Hooper—three. Castillo—zero.

The scribbled scorecard had been taped to his flight monitor. The hand on his back told him that agent Harley Hooper, Charley 1's pilot, had walked into his trailer.

"Enrique, my man. You lost big time last week. Charley 1. Three solid bustolas. All significant drug intercepts. Two boats. One box truck. And a goose egg for you, amigo. You were a loser, except for your four BOD points...your Babes on Decks sightings. You owe me fifty-bucks, buddy."

Enrique pulled out his wallet and counted out the cash. "Yeah, you were lucky. When I sent the federales after some trucks, they were from a local rock quarry."

"Well, fifty bucks says I beat your ass again next week," said Hooper.

"Fifty? Make it a hundred."

"You got that. You know, Enrique, I hate to take your GrandeBurger money. Lorena's might have to go out of business."

Enrique was suffering. Overly sensitive about the strange bumps on Charley 2, he kept explaining to his colleagues about the otherworldly forces that may be reaching out to us. In return for his candor, he became the fodder for office jokes. Someone kept posting pictures of flying saucers on his locker. His co-workers were calling him E.T. Castillo, captain of the alien fleet. A copy of Jody Foster's movie *Contact*, about interaction with other planets, landed on his desk. The Captain continually warned him to pay attention to the fishing boats and the shorelines and forget the little green spacemen. Now, his drug bust totals were down and, worst of all, he had stopped low-flying the beaches while searching for skinny dippers.

His personal life was also a mess. Long-time girlfriend Sylvia used to be fascinated by his rough-and-tumble stories about chasing drug gangs through the desert. She revved up on his dramatic retellings and cooked savory dinners to celebrate the action-packed busts. Sylvia would sit for hours, listening raptly as he turned routine foot chases in between the cactus into dangerous pursuits. She roared delightedly when Enrique or "QuiQue" as she called him, finally got the cuffs on a miscreant. Her uptick in adrenaline encouraged more playfulness. The couple would enjoy sweaty re-enactments of the captures, playing a game called Ofelia: Naughty Narco Queen of the Desert, sometimes rampaging in the buff around the apartment jumping on furniture, sometimes she would stand there naked while he held a toy pistol on her and searched her, sometimes he would bind her in the hand-cuffs she found in one of those adult stores, all of it ending with shrieking and cavorting in his bedroom while she coyly begged him not to "take her down to the office."

But then Captain Dolan offered agent Castillo a chance to join the Predator Program and become an air interdiction pilot-agent for the drones.

The cavorting in the apartment dried up. While he took classes at Holloman Air Force Base in New Mexico, he didn't see Sylvia for weeks. During the weekends they did spend together, Enrique chattered on about instruction manuals and flying the drone. This did not stimulate her playfulness. Sylvia was bored. She would roll her eyes.

"All you do is sit on your ass and wiggle your joystick. It's not very dangerous. And you are getting fat," Sylvia complained.

Enrique was put out. "It's the same. I'm getting busts."

"No, it's not the same. It's chickenshit. It's like cowboys flying helicopters to herd cattle."

"What are you talking about? Drones are the future."

"But it's so boring. It's not exciting like the running around you used to do. You are getting soft. You don't have any more scary stories. Now we play "Enrique the Aguila —the Eagle" and I'm no longer Queen Ofelia. All I get to do now is watch you pump your rudder pedals and twiddle your joystick. Really."

"Sylvia, you don't understand."

"Oh, I do. And I'm bored with all this."

She let loose her Hellfire missile.

"I've been meaning to tell you. When you were gone

for so long, I think I met somebody. He's a deputy sheriff who saves people's lives."

Enrique was stunned. "What are you saying?"

"I think...QuiQue...I think you should see other people too."

"You're kidding."

"No, not kidding."

And that was that. No dinner that night. No hand-cuffs. No rampaging through the apartment naked playing Naughty Narco Queen Ofelia. No steamy sex. She just picked up her jacket and left. One week later, she came for her stuff while he was at work.

For Enrique, time now passed in slow motion. The sudden breakup smacked his self-esteem pretty hard. He moped around the office and stopped going out for Friday night pizza with the drone maintenance gang. For several weeks, he tried seeing a psychologist recommended by the Captain. But after two sessions, the therapist chided Castillo for his morose self-pity, saying that he needed to stop whining and get back in the fray. "So she left you. It could happen to anyone. Take it like a man and get on it with it. Try to improve your life."

Enrique took that advice to heart. He signed up again at a local gym. But getting on the treadmill seemed like a lot of effort—so he stopped going.

He joined chat rooms for singles, pouring out his troubles to a snarky on-line social advisor named Luisa. At first she offered consolation and suggestions to turn around his dismal social forays. But that avenue of solace turned sour when he happened upon her one day in a café in Yuma and discovered she wasn't twenty something, like her picture, but seventy-one and using a walker.

He dove into a dozen self-help books. His favorite *Twenty-one Ways to be a Man Again* seemed to fit his situation perfectly. Change your furniture. Try a new haircut.

He started to get a tattoo. On his shoulder blade. A Mexican eagle with a drone in its talons. But the needle hurt so much he never went back for the second sitting. So now, the half-finished drone nose cone, looking like a banana in the clutches of a chicken, decorated his back.

Dating? Enrique only knew about family gatherings. His sporadic expeditions to singles bars were fruitless. The tough border agent who might wrestle with gun-carrying narco-traffickers was a shy, withdrawn soul in club scene. The conversations always went dead when the women asked him what he did. Of course he was reluctant to talk about his job; he considered it top secret. Instead, he would tell them he was in the space program, training for a mission to Mars. It only took ten minutes in the presence of any woman before the ersatz astronaut Enrique would begin whining about Sylvia, a self-indulgent monologue that continued until his new dating prospect ran screaming out of the restaurant.

Oprah reruns had touted a testosterone boosting diet by a Dr. Jean-Paul Fleury. Go vegan and this regimen would treat worry and depression while raising the libido. He tried that for a few days but became bored, hungry and anxious that it wouldn't work. So he gave up, returning to a routine of buying the super bacon deluxe GrandeBurger and fries at Lorena's Burger Adobe on his way home and eating that artery-clogging meal while he played solo rounds of golf on his video game.

The lonely days wore on. With Sylvia contentedly enjoying Hide the Suspect with her deputy sheriff, Agent Enrique Castillo gave up on the *Twenty-one Ways to be a Man*. Instead, all he did was go to work, fly Charley 2, and sit on his ass.

5

Pepe Draws Them In

"Spectacular. This giant manta ray is a welcome gift from God," said Padre Nacho. He and the ejido boss Gabriela Cortez had driven out to the shoreline at Punta Gringa. "What do you call him?"

"Pepe," she said. "He's a certified tourist draw."

"You are so lucky. How long will he stay?"

"He's been here two weeks. We hope forever."

Pepe the manta ray had adopted Playa Refugio. His playful breaches and gyrations in the offshore waters inspired cautious optimism about a tourist boom in the isolated village. Twice as many visitors were rolling in and staying over. The El Parador Motel and Eco-Camp was nearly booked solid, the first time that had happened in 25 years. The Acosta grocery store was making a killing, selling tee-shirts, sweatpants, swim trunks and baseball caps with a goofy manta ray logo. The pangueros had given up on fishing and were busy hauling tourists out to watch his antics.

Padre Nacho was in town in his role as the prime tub-thumper for the East Baja coastline. Often, to ensure the tourist machinery worked well, the Padre dispensed blessings. Last month, he staged a ceremony for Mexicali's fleet of taco trucks, praying that divine intervention would reduce the food-borne diseases from the ptomaine-prone mobile kitchens. So far on this trip, he blessed the credit card reader at the Dos Cacti mini-golf course and the Pancho Villa statue that took orders at Drive-Thru Tacos in San Felipe, and finally the new wine and beer cooler at the Acosta grocery in Refugio.

The Bishop had tried to rein him in, but if it involved tourism, Padre Nacho was a force. Today at noon, under a crystal clear blue sky, the Padre was to officially bless the new life-size statue of Pepe, the giant manta ray. The ejido's youthful faction decided the village needed a roadside mascot. They commissioned fiberglass expert and sandspit rata Eliot to build the replica. Now it sat on the bed of a stake truck, waiting for its journey to its permanent base at the road turnoff.

The television crews were rolling as the Padre, having donned a Pepe the Manta Ray tee-shirt, baseball cap, shorts and running shoes, placed a hand-woven religious stole around his neck and gingerly climbed atop the replica ray. The padre produced a small cup of water, blessed it, and sprinkled it on the statue.

"We are gathered to recognize the visit of this wonderful animal. He is ours to behold. May this statue serve as a reminder to us that we are the stewards of this land and ocean and that we should do everything we can to protect all from harm. Oh Lord, bless this statue that it may inspire the tourists to come to our parched land and to stay many days as possible at our motels and eat plenty of fish tacos at our restaurants."

The cameras loved it. The crews interviewed the Padre, a couple of weathered pangueros, Gabriela Cortez and the Acosta brothers, who had ponied up the pesos for the statue. Merc took photos and uploaded the comments to his anti-pollution blog. Eliot, the sculptor, was nowhere to be seen.

The Padre sensed he could milk this further. After all, the television jackals needed action video. He cornered several pangueros and begged for a ride out to see Pepe. The entourage went down to the silted-up harbor and managed to find enough gas to fire up four pangas to take the priest and his paparazzi onto the water.

Pepe was in good form, breaching every five minutes or so. Like a skateboarder, the youthful fish had devised exotic aerial twists and rolls to please the growing audience. When the Padre arrived at the scene off Punta Gringa, there were already 15 kayaks filled with tourists in the water.

"What a joy. What a joyful beast," said Padre Macho Nacho, watching the giant manta ray cavort and splash near the kayak flotilla, spraying seawater onto the amused visitors. The goal here was intimacy, getting tourists as close as possible to the huge creature. So far, there had been no accidents, although if a kayak floated into the wrong spot, the manta's one-ton bulk, floppy wings and youthful exuberance could slap a kayaker silly.

"Why does he stay here?" asked the Padre.

Antonio, the local marine biologist with him in the

panga, shrugged. "We know he likes the underwater hot springs that reach out from Punta Gringa canyon. The warmer water combines with the runoff from La Gringa's goat farm to generate an unending source of his favorite food—plankton. Actually, scientists have seen this manta before, down by Cabo. We tagged him and we've followed him by satellite. He's one of the smartest mantas I've seen. He's really a mooch."

"A mooch? You mean a beggar?"

"A very smart one. He will only jump near the kayaks where the pangueros bring him tasty buckets of chum. He's taught the pangueros to scoop up the slimy stuff near Punta Gringa and bring loads of it out to where he does his performances."

"So, he is training us," the Padre said.

"Absolutely," said Antonio. "He did the same thing in Cabo. And, he still has spots on his back so he's a pup. In human terms, we'd call him a teenager. How long will be stay in these waters? Maybe when it is time to mate, he'll head back south to Cabo to find a girlfriend. We have no idea. He seems to be having a good time and he's got us just where he wants us."

The video crews loved the shots on the water. They hunted for others to interview while they bobbed at sea. Doc and Merc had joined the armada in the *Outta Here*. Wearing a tee-shirt with an outline of a U.S. Predator drone on the front with a red diagonal line through it, Doc introduced himself as one of the first to see the manta when it showed up offshore. The cameras began a boat-to-boat interview.

"We were shocked when he leaped from the water.

It seemed half the Sea of Cortez landed in our boat. Seeing such a large creature is a humbling experience. And that was just before we saw the drone crash into the desert," Doc said.

The reporters weren't sure how this related but Doc was not going to stop. He went on to describe graphically how the crippled drone tumbled through the sky and crashed. He claimed they had to extinguish a flaming inferno fueled by the volatile aviation gas. He was on his message, spurred by a hatred of the air force and its medical benefit program. Finally, one by one, the reporters excused themselves and turned to others to juice up the manta ray story.

Merc maneuvered the *Outta Here* away from the cameras. "Doc, you've got to stop that drone bullshit. I know you hate the air force, but it's only going to cause us trouble."

"What trouble? Merc, they deserve it."

"Doc, there have been people down here in Refugio that I haven't seen before. They aren't tourists and they haven't come here to see Pepe leap. These are agents. Three-day beards and body armor. I get very nervous when people like that are around."

"Well."

"We really don't want strangers wandering around in Gringa."

"I'm not worried. I've got nothing to hide."

"But others do. Desperate criminals in these hills want things to stay nice and quiet. So, don't rock the boat. You're a fool if you don't shut up."

"If you feel that way, then go screw yourself. I don't

want to talk to you." And Doc refused to speak to Merc for days. He stopped inviting him to the poker games.

Then Doc and his longtime lover Rose began getting thickly accented anonymous phone calls with a very clear message—he needed to shut or else. Doc laughed these off. He had patched up the broken bodies of soldiers in wars. He was tough. He had guns. He didn't scare easily.

One day last week, Doc went missing.

6

Doc's Demise

As Merc walked up, Ruby was sitting on his welcome mat, arms wrapped around her knees, gazing up at a starlit night sky and smoking a joint. She never looked over at him. "Hey. I should warn you. Shay's in there and she's got a gun."

"A gun? Shay? A gun?"

"Shay. A gun. That's what I said. Little tiny Shay. Big old gun." Ruby pointed her finger at him and with a child-like gesture, pantomimed pulling a trigger. "Like ka-pow." She paused for a second. "I think it's loaded…and I'm not joking."

"Tell me you used your deputy sheriff training to get it away from her."

"Those skills are retired, good buddy." Ruby took a long hit on the joint. "I'm nearly fifty and fat and one of those jolly brown Filipinas who no longer respond to suspect with weapon calls. Besides, Merc, it's your shack." Ruby stubbed the joint out on the doorframe. "You are going to have to deal with little Shay and her studly .45."

The already stifling Mexican night sure felt a lot warmer. *Here we go,* he thought. *It's up to me again.* Mercury Stiles, the de facto ringleader for the declining population of ex-pat recluses on the Punta Gringa sandspit, was about to wade into another wrenching session with his closest neighbors.

Everyone was still in shock about the news. The San Felipe police identified a corpse they found 48 hours ago as the missing sandspit resident Will Tedford, known to all his friends as Doc. No one had seen him for days until the body appeared next to a burned out shack at a road junction north of Playa Refugio. Violent crime was now on everyone's mind. Paranoia was strangling their laid-back community.

Merc knocked cautiously. "Hey Shay. I'm back. Don't shoot."

Shay answered from inside. "Hey, kiddo. Sorry Ruby and I barged in. Hope you don't mind that we helped ourselves to snacks."

At least, at least she sounded rational. *A good sign,* he thought. With Ruby right behind him, Merc made a cautious step across the threshold into his one-room home. An oil lamp spread a dim yellow glow around the kitchen table where Shay sat drinking a beer and nibbling on tortillas and salsa. There was no gun in sight. Shay had bloodshot eyes, had been crying. "I heard the cartel tweaks popped Doc in the head before lighting him up. What kind of animals are they?" Shay didn't wait for an answer. "Merc. Merc. Sorry. I've always thought Gringa or even San Felipe was safe. Safe. That those news stories about crazy drug murders were hype. I've always told people to drive on down to visit. I think people are basically good. But this stupid killing really scares the shit out of me."

Venting is good. Get it out of your system. Rage if you want. He owed it to her. As skittish and half-crazy as Shay often was, she was an anchor to the quirky Punta Gringa social community. Despite Doc's medical background, Shay had assumed the role as self-appointed health guru, maintaining a list of local doctors, shamans, curanderas, brujas, unlicensed chiropractors, quacks, mystics, massage therapists, and herbalists. Traumas from jellyfish stings, scorpion encounters, cactus spines, sun poisoning, and tainted water—she had the answers. And, she was a neighbor, often sensible but just as often filled with rage.

"Rose is gone too," said Shay. "Doc loved Rose so much and never was abusive, like most men I have hooked up with. Like my vile ex-husband. Even through those two were younger than us oldies, they were as inseparable as any sweethearts. Once she heard the news about the Doc's body being found, she took off."

"This is just so weird," said Ruby.

Shay sat back down. "This place. This crappy isolated sandspit. Punta Gringa always has been such a safe hideaway. What a shock. Someone really bad is out of control and it's dangerous now."

Merc tried to calm her. "I know this is....".

Shay only glared at him. "Merc. Am I the only smart one?" She pulled the pistol from her purse. "I'm ready."

Merc stepped back. "Yeah, Ruby said you were packing. Where in the hell did you get that .45? You know the

Mexicans aren't keen on guns. They'll throw you in jail if they find it. And if it's loaded, please put it away."

Shay rested her elbow on the table and aimed the gun barrel at the ceiling. "Yes it's loaded. With hollow points. After I heard he was shot, I went over to Rose and Doc's house, opened his fake wall and snatched this Colt. And the ammo."

Shay was a wisp. Slender. Less than five feet tall. Born in Morocco, her skin was the color of café ole. Her sleeveless shirts exposed well-defined biceps and a pair of snake tattoos that encircled her right arm like a caduceus. Her mouth could tighten when angry. She wouldn't take crap from anyone.

Ruby pushed Shay's arm until the gun barrel pointed toward the wall. "Shay, watch the hell where you point that. Do you even know how to shoot that thing?"

Waving the heavy handgun, she turned toward Ruby. "Sure. Two months ago, Doc taught me how to use this very pistola."

"Where?"

"Out by the old mines. Doc said he was getting ready for something, so we spent days shooting up a bunch of cactus."

"And you used that .45? Little you?" asked Ruby.

"I had no problem. In fact," and Shay smiled, "I get off on the recoil."

"Shay. Please put it away. You know I carried my duty weapon for twenty years but never fired it outside the pistol range."

"So, you never shot anyone?"

"No. Never. In all those years. Yeah, sometimes I had

to point it at the perps to emphasize that I meant business, but I never pulled the trigger. Thank god I didn't
have to. I never wanted to kill. Never wanted to put bullets into anyone."

Shay turned and waved the gun toward Merc. "Well,
I'd do it now. I will follow the old saying—If you pull the
gun...you'd better pull the trigger. No killer will mess with
me now. I'll blow their frigging head off. You, Merc, you
ever shoot anyone?"

"No comment," said Merc, turning his back.

Shay was delighted. "Wow. You must have. I bet you
did. You must have killed someone. Probably in the air
force. Maybe you shot a general who pissed you off.
Those must be deep dark secrets. I know."

Shay stuck the Colt in her purse.

Ruby turned to Merc. "So, what more do you know?"

He took out a notebook. "Well, okay. The federales
said Doc was shot in the side of the head but that the
body was pretty badly messed up in the fire. They showed
me a wallet and his dog tags. They were Doc's all right."

Ruby looked puzzled. "Are they sure it was Doc? Did
they do any forensics? An autopsy? Who identified the
body?"

"They didn't say. But Doc's wallet was there—minus
any money. And don't forget the dog tags."

"Well. Here's a question. Why would some tweak kill
him and then burn up the body? And leave the wallet?
Maybe the cops have it wrong."

Merc wrapped his homemade salsa in a tortilla. He
took a sip from a beer. "We can hope it was a mistake.
Maybe he's still alive. Maybe it was something more sin-

ister. Doc wasn't exactly a saint. I mean...he could be aggressive toward people. Piss them off. He pissed me off a lot. Especially when he had a few too many beers. You know, he wasn't even speaking to me when he disappeared. Maybe he had a darker side he kept from us. After all, he hid weapons all over Rose's house."

Shay began softly weeping again. Ruby put her arm around Shay's shoulder. "Oh, honey, I know this is hard." Ruby paused to open a beer. "This whole thing is a wake-up call. Us gals have our freedom to live alone in Punta Gringa. Men here can be violent to independent women. You know I have my rifle. We have to be as tough as anyone. If we can't defend ourselves, if it gets too crazy down here, we should shoot first and then get the hell out of here."

"No shit," said Shay.

"But most of all, sisters should stick together. Fight for each other," said Ruby.

Merc got up. For the moment, he didn't quite know what to do with these agitated women friends. Sisters with guns. Neighbors ready to pull the trigger. His dad had been a hunter and he had lived his life with guns in the house. After his brother was shot to death as a teenager, he hated weapons. He could still handle them but he would rather leave them be and walk away.

"Excuse me, ladies. I need air." He walked outside, letting the screen door bang against the jamb, and stood for a moment on the sketchy road that wound through the underbrush. He kicked off his sandals and stubbed his feet into the cool sand.

At that moment, the familiar "ka-thump" of Playa Refugio's diesel electricity generator echoed across the desert. It was shutting down at nine o'clock. The village lights two miles to the north faded from sparkling to a primal blackness. Now the land was dead quiet again. The faint glow from a fingernail moon barely lit up the mesquite bushes, the RVs, rusting trailers, sandy beach and ramshackle houses. He could hear Pepe splashing around offshore, carrying on in the darkness.

Usually the rich bought this kind of peace in their gated seaside condos but at the Punta Gringa enclave, tranquility came with the rough edges of the place. That's why the desert rats like Merc could put up with gun crazy neighbors. The stillness was the payoff. This is all he wanted. To be left alone. The emptiness made life bearable.

7

The Memorial

Dolan dreaded the next twenty minutes he would spend with the nuttiest of his drone pilots. He expected more weird ideas, fueled by the grease from Castillo's fast-food diet and his growing sexual starvation.

Okay, I'll face it. I'll listen to his crazy theories about aliens and spacemen attacking his drone. I swear to god, these drone fliers are pussies. Dolan opened his office door and Castillo quickly strode inside.

"Thanks for seeing me. I want to apologize for my lack of busts lately."

"What's up? More UFOs?" asked Dolan.

Enrique ignored the sarcasm. "No. But remember how Charley 2 vibrated two days ago and we couldn't find anything wrong?"

"Yeah."

"The same as it did last week?"

"That's what you are telling everyone."

Castillo dramatically laid out a dozen 8 x 10 color photos of Charley 2 on the Captain's desk. "Well, I was right. The maintenance boys did a second check last night using black lamps and found these marks on top of the Predator's fuselage. One is next to the wing root; the other is up front by the avionics tray. Slight indentations where the surface is scratched. It's probably the same attacker that brought down Charley 3 two weeks ago."

"Castillo, that drone had engine failure. Pure and simple."

"That's not what people think. Or what we know."

Dolan absentmindedly thumbed through the photos.

"And you are saying something landed on Charley 2 in these exact spots?"

"We don't know. But it sure is odd."

Dolan looked carefully at a closeup of the radar pod. "These marks could be almost anything, Castillo. Charley 2 is an old Middle East war bird. He's been bumped and banged many times. These spots could even be turkey vulture poop from our own flight line. So," and Captain Dolan leaned back in his chair, "anything else different about Charley 2? Did you run diagnostics on the telemetry."

"Yeah, and everything checks out. It's just doesn't make sense," said Castillo.

Why, oh why, did I inherit this collection of weirdos? "Okay, well, watch him very carefully when he is up today. If there's any sign of another bump, I'll have a look. Oh, and by the way, Iris and her buddies that you busted over a week ago…they're back on the street again. They got probation. And the Mexicans kept the boat."

"Well, that's the way…"

"And Enrique. I know you are addicted to these UFO conspiracies and things. And I know you've been going through tough personal problems. And I know your girlfriend...well...if you don't mind me saying so, she was a weird one. So her throwing you over might have been a blessing. And I'm sorry about that. But a domestic mess like you've got can take it out of a person. Distract him. Lead to ill-considered decisions. I know you are under stress. If you want some time off or something, say so."

"I'm fine, Captain."

"Well, think about it. You could take a week. Or more. Go to someplace where it's cool." *Go to someplace away from here and me,* he thought.

"No, I'm okay."

"Then stick with it. Remember the sterling record of your father, Edgar Castillo, the toughest border agent ever. He never let one setback keep him from doing his job. He was out busting bad guys every day for forty years."

"I'll remember that, Captain."

That's right. They would never let Enrique forget his dad Edgar, known as *El Toro*—the Bull—the consummate border agent who retired after four decades of tough, dusty fieldwork. His father had more arrests than any other agent who ever worked for the Border Protection. Three Presidential citations. Fifteen straight years as the top agent in the Southwest district. His autobiography, *Steel Bull in the Desert,* laced with epic confrontations against the drug traffickers, stayed sixty weeks on the *New York Times* bestseller list. The legend of Edgar Castillo, hero to all border agents, exemplar of the non-complainers, would forever cloud Enrique's days, especially in the Yuma office. After all, who could avoid seeing papa El Toro's knowing smile eternally gazing down from a movie-poster-sized oil portrait on the wall, where it occupied a holy space next to the photo of the President.

Yes, he—Enrique—was the legacy hire. He got into agent training with the Customs and Border Protection service because, well, they had to find him a job. Hiring Enrique the son kept El Toro the father from retiring the last few years. But Enrique was fine with that. He had work and enough money to dine in style every night at Lorena's Burger Adobe on South Fourth Street.

Enrique headed back to the flight console in his trailer. His Predator stood ready on the tarmac with its preflight complete. At his signal, the crew chief removed the wheel chocks. Castillo wiggled the rudder pedals, and moved to the run-up pad. Departure control cleared him and he turned onto the runway and advanced the throttle.

These takeoffs were always magical. Charley 2 buzzed down the runway, accelerating as Enrique softly pulled back on the joystick, lifting off and gently climbing into the Arizona sky. Now he was a pilot once again and, as the poet said, breaking the surly bonds of earth. Reaching six hundred feet, he started a slow turn toward Mexico. *Let's see what surprises are out there today. Maybe more babes on the sailboats.*

Heading south, the outskirts of Mexicali passed quickly. Soon he was over the coastline at San Felipe. The air at ten thousand feet was rough, but he didn't want to take Charley 2 higher because visibility with the hi-resolution cameras was best beneath the cloud layers.

A short time and he was cruising above the Playa

Refugio fishing harbor, where he saw a substantial crowd standing out in the open. *What the fuck*, he thought. *That's very unusual for this two-bit village.*

—⚒—

Merc daydreamed as he watched the spindly silver plane slip across the sky darting in and out of the puffy clouds. Another damn drone, another el mosco. Maybe the first one had something to do with Doc's murder. He had warned him to shut up.

But back to the task at hand. It was ten on a June morning and the thermometer had already busted the century mark. Two hundred locals were baking in the sunlight, milling around in Playa Refugio's treeless municipal dirt parking lot, waiting for the Doc's celebration of life service. Even some confused tourists straggled in, looking for the manta ray Pepe.

The turnout pleased Merc. Organizing this had not been easy. In a tiny fishing harbor like Playa Refugio, there was no precedent. No one could remember the last memorial for a foreigner in Playa Refugio. For that matter, no one could remember a memorial for anyone in the village.

That's because no one wanted to die in this backwater. Patients with terminal illnesses did everything they could not to expire in Playa Refugio. The humiliation would be an eternal smudge on one's legacy. Departing this life while stuck in the middle of nowhere was the ultimate insult.

So which Mexicans to invite? The scorpion lady Señora Cortez was a slam dunk. Then there was the top political star in the local constellation, District Delegado Eduardo Arce of San Felipe, who once tried to have Doc thrown in the slammer? Or his wife, Elena, who pitched a drink in Doc's face at the yearly New Year's Eve fest after he had affectionately positioned his palm on her behind? Or the district fish inspector, Dr. Pablo Rosales, who made a habit of routinely fining Doc for casting from the shore without a license? Or Mexican Marine Captain Jose Onte, who once lost substantially to Doc in the weekly poker game and then had his soldiers roughly search his long-time partner Rose's house, claiming he suspected Doc of running a drug ring.

In the end, Merc simply put up notices all over town: at the fresh water spring, Acosta's grocery store, the ejido office, the El Parador Motel and Eco-Camp, the boat launching ramp, the Loncheria La Pasadita, the village sub-delegado's office, and the parking lot. *Let folks sort it out themselves*, he thought.

Choosing the location had been simple. The Punta Gringa sandspit lacked a gathering spot, so Playa Refugio was it. And because the little fishing village had no church, no chapel, no community center or beer warehouse spacious enough for an indoor service and the grim town plaza was overrun with red ants and dead plants, the only outdoor venue suitable was the municipal office's barren unpaved parking lot.

Merc had spruced up the site with blowups of Rose and Doc wearing their trademark wraparound sunglasses. These were taped to the non-functioning ambulance on blocks beside the sub-delegado's office. Shay drove outside of town and retrieved clusters of fragrant desert lilies, now in bloom, along with ocotillos and desert marigolds; she arranged these in white five-gallon buckets. For a sound system, Merc borrowed Alan the Croatian's guitar amplifier and speaker, pirated a microphone from the delegacion and hooked the whole system into the town electrical grid.

Ruby rehearsed the amateur singing group for the music. Calling themselves the Daughters of Joyful Light, they entered in a single file from behind the auto repair shack, sweating visibly in their home-made robes made of sailcloth salvaged from the *Delighted Carnality,* a sixty-foot yacht that ran aground after a drug bust two years before. The choir members gathered around the microphone.

"This little light of mine...
I'm going to let it shine.
All over Playa Refugio,
I'm gonna let it shine...
Let it shine, let it shine, let it shine."

The Daughters switched into Spanish for *La Golondrina,* the traditional lament for a migrant who didn't make it back to home.

"*A donde irá veloz y fatigada
la golondrina que de aquí se va.
No tiene cielo, te mira angustiada sin
paz ni abrigo que la vio partir*"

Then in English for the foreign residents who never did learn Spanish.

"Where will it go—swift and weary—
The swallow that's gone away on a journey.
If in the wind she finds herself astray
Seeking shelter so far away."

Padre Macho Nacho had driven down to Refugio in his dusty old pickup to remember a good friend with whom he had worked for years, coordinating the Flying Medics clinic program.

Merc invited him despite their differences. The Padre's aggressive push for jobs had been the decisive support behind the battery recycling plant that now menaced the sandspit residents. The Padre argued that locating it in Gringa kept the plant's lead pollution away from the Mexican children who lived in the Playa Refugio village, that the area needed the jobs and that because the plant had to go somewhere, so why not Punta Gringa?

Padre Nacho had another reason for showing up. Stories of mass graves and headless victims in a drug war continually blazed across the tabloids. The Padre wanted to calm fears and emphasize that Doc's tragedy was an isolated event. He had to reassure the tourists. He was wearing a Pepe the Giant Manta tee-shirt.

When the singers finished, the padre stepped to the microphone and asked for silence. He spoke in Spanish first and then English. "We want to thank the Daughters of Joyful Light. That was the beautiful song *La Golondrina*. You know it remembers travelers far from home. Even so, I wonder if Doc might have disagreed. I know he considered Playa Refugio, this humble village of sanctuary, to be his home."

"We gather on this warm spring day to remember a

fine member of our community. He was very loving. Very respectful. A great poker player. Full of fun. It's true that he was a foreigner, but Doc worked hard to bring free health care from the Flying Medics to the less fortunate. His random death on a remote back country road was tragic. It is hard for us to understand how God would let something as violent as this happen to a good person. Tourists who seek out our motels and kayak rentals know this violence was a random event and that our highways are safe. Doc was a part of our daily lives. May his soul rest in peace."

The crowd murmured "Amen".

The Padre continued. "Many have asked to say a few words about Doc."

Gabriela spoke first.

"Doc is gone, rest his soul, and we also lost his partner Rose. We dearly loved these strong, independent foreigners. Doc and Rose worked tirelessly to see that people in this village got health care from the Flying Medics. These were two people who made the effort to speak Spanish and were welcomed by many families in our village. We will miss them terribly."

Merc was touched by the Señora's compassionate tone. It was hard to imagine that this tough woman had a softer side.

Merc was up next. "Merc Stiles here representing the foreign residents who love this village. I want to say that Doc's passing leaves a gaping hole in the hearts of all here. Doc had a great affection for the people of Playa Refugio. I know that Doc took many fishing trips with the local fishermen. His weekly poker games were a delight.

He loved the purity of the desert and he loved Rose."
Merc choked up so he placed the microphone back on its
stand and sat down.

Shay approached. Wearing shorts, a tee-shirt and a
floppy straw hat, she clutched a Pacifico beer tightly in
her right hand and carried her .45 in her shoulder bag.
There were tears in her eyes.

"I had a dream this morning...dreamed that Doc was
here, watching his own funeral. So I guess I'm not a real-
ist." Shay wiped her eyes. "How could anyone be so cruel
to kill such a good man? We all adored Doc. He was
cranky at times, but we loved him. He was the kindest
person in the world, innocently burned up in violence that
we cannot understand. But Doc is gone. His light is out.
His flame extinguished."

Francisco Arcangel spoke next. He was the respected manager of the Bat-Mex Renewal S.A. battery recycling plant. An engineer trained in Mexico City, he had
hired over thirty local Refugians to work in his factory,
outfitting each with the latest protective jumpsuits and
respirators. The building had the most advanced environmental scrubbers and Arcangel had challenged anyone,
including the ex-pat yahoos like Merc on the sandspit
across the road, to find dangerous lead pollution outside
the plant. No surveys had turned up any.

"I know I speak for all. We knew Doc and respected
him. Yes, Doc fought hard against my plant but he staged
a clean and respectful campaign. When he could find no
pollution, he admitted that. I admired him for that. I also
honor him for his work with the Flying Medics. What
could be more valuable to the local people than bringing

in medical care when it is out of reach for our little community? In his honor, the Bat-Mex Renewal Company will donate one hundred thousand pesos, that's ten thousand dollars, to the Flying Medics program." The crowd applauded.

Merc scoffed. Arcangel was just too perfect. He oozed insincerity. Something smelled fishy.

While Arcangel was at the microphone, Merc had scanned the crowd. He counted three known drug agents from both the Mexican and U.S. governments, clean-shaven younger men with crew cuts and bulging shirts covering Kevlar vests. Everyone's favorite cartel scout Iris Lopez stood in the back, mixed in with the ordinary folks.

There was a tall figure in dark glasses, cowboy boots and a black western tailored shirt. He had been standing in front of Merc. "Doc should have seen this," he said to the man beside him. This puzzling character had an unfamiliar Spanish accent, very rapid with its words slurred together and plurals skipped entirely. Not Mexican. Merc searched his brain to recall where he had heard that accent before. It was the Cuban warehouseman at the marine engine parts store in Arizona. But a Cuban here? You have as much chance of finding a Cuban in Playa Refugio as finding a Martian.

By now, the Daughters of Joyful Light had shed their clammy choir robes and were fanning themselves with their hats. They gathered to warble through their closing hymn—a confused rendition of Amazing Grace. The well-dressed Cuban finished chatting with his friend. At that point, he walked up to Merc, nodded respectfully, and spoke in Spanish. "Please accept my condolences on the death of your friend. You should know that my group would not be involved in the death of anyone who works for the benefit of the village. If we catch the animals who did this, they will suffer a terrible, terrible fate."

Before Merc could answer, the stranger walked away. Merc shuddered. No doubt about it. This was a cartel speaking. It's good to know they weren't the ones who murdered Doc. Still, he had to steer clear of this man. Expats had no business getting anywhere near known narco traffickers.

Merc had to be smart about this. Doc had once let on to Merc that he had a quid pro quo connection with Cubans. Something about finishing a deal he had made. So even if the cartel didn't have a hand in Doc's death, Merc knew he might run into the Cuban again. He didn't relish that. At this point in his life, Merc's solution to conflict was to hit the road. Having this Cuban dispute hang over his head was unnerving. Once again, even while dead, Doc had pissed him off.

8

RJ Joins the Fight

Shay awoke shivering. She had fallen asleep atop her covers to escape the stifling June heat. But in the dead of night, a haze rose over the sea and a breeze off the water blew damp salty air into her rustic trailer.

She tossed and turned but gave up. Time to seek out some warmth. Pulling on a tee-shirt, Shay wrapped herself in a kimono, put the .45 in the pocket and set out barefoot onto the cold sand along the road. Sunrise was an hour away, but a pink morning glow lit up the sandspit.

Shay let herself in the front door of Merc's one room shack. He was snoring in a bed pushed against the wall. In the darkness, Shay tripped over his boots.

"Who?" said Merc.

"It's Shay, kiddo." She stood over his bed, took off the kimono, sat on the covers and brushed the sand off her feet.

"Shay, what the hell?"

"Merc, I'm cold and lonesome. You're a great warm friend. So I had to tell you. I had this dream. Doc is still alive. I dreamed Doc walked back into town. And you know, dreams really do mean something."

"Yeah, right. I'd like to believe that too…but it's a bit, just a bit unrealistic."

"Well, wouldn't that be the best outcome? Doc returns." She finished cleaning her feet and turned toward Merc. "Right now, I need to be with somebody. Can I sit here for a while?"

Merc had barely opened his eyes. "Sure, no problem but it's way early. Think I'm gonna sleep a bit longer."

"Go ahead. I just need to be near someone who is sad."

"Sad. Sure." And Merc drifted back to sleep.

Shay shook him awake. "Merc. Don't you feel empty? Doc was your fishing buddy. Your poker buddy."

"Yeah, but he got pissed and wouldn't talk to me. He could drive you nuts."

"So you guys weren't talking when he went missing."

"Yeah. That's too bad. Now, he's just gone."

"And you and I didn't get a chance to say goodbye."

"It's true. He's just flat-assed gone—not in our lives anymore."

"Well, the murder scares me. Rose heading off alone scares me. Merc, I need someone now. I'm lonesome and drained. Do you mind if I climb under the covers?"

Merc opened one eye. "Mostly, you want a warm body. Sure, yeah sure. But no funny stuff."

Still wearing her tee-shirt, Shay crawled over Merc

and snuggled with her back to the wall. Her chilly thighs were like cold pipes pressing against his. "I'm lonely. Let's grieve for Doc together. Give me a hug."

Merc didn't budge. "Hey, it's too early for a hug. Besides, you know what that will lead to."

"Hey, kiddo, this is just a hug. I'm not horny. A simple hug doesn't have to lead to sweaty passion."

"Well, you're in my bed in a tee-shirt and various parts are touching and it normally leads to that, and when it happens, it happens."

Shay feigned a shocked attitude. "It happens?"

"I don't know. I'm half-asleep, for chrissakes."

"Merc, you always amaze me. I mean you really amaze me. I mean right now in Punta Gringa you have women who adore you, but instead, you are forever going to the mute whore in Refugio."

"I would prefer to discuss this later. Can I please get some sleep?"

"No. It's time to talk about Magdalena."

"What makes you think I know someone named Magdalena?"

"Kiddo, it's no secret. Gossip, Merc. We're a tight community. Maggie, or Senorita No Speak as we gringas here call her, is always a visitor out here on the first Sunday night each month. We know you bring her out here."

"Okay. So what. It's great fun without any...any complications."

"But you also know that if you need it—the basic passion experience—well you can come to me any time.

I don't mind. It would save you some money. Of course, I'm not talking about right now."

"Shay, the basic passion experience? This is nuts."

"No, I'm serious."

"Shay. We're good friends."

"That hasn't stopped us before."

"Okay. I'll take a rain check. Now can I sleep?"

"Suit yourself. Right now I just want to be close."

"Shay."

She gave him a kiss on his check and said, "Kiddo. I don't understand why? Why do friends die? Doc…Doc is just gone."

"Doc didn't know when to shut up. He should have fucking shut up. I was mad at him, but I'll really miss him."

Merc reached out and scratched Shay's spiky hair. She drifted off. She was breathing softly and it was peaceful with her asleep in his arms. He never had to worry. Shay had an equally powerful fear of close relationships.

Merc never went back to sleep. Instead, he lay thinking of Doc, and through the east window, he watched a red sun climb out of the haze over the Sea of Cortez.

—∞—

Outside, RJ enjoyed the daybreak from the canvas chair on his trailer's mini-porch, where he sat reading from his Old Testament. The traditional stories always cheered him up, and their straightforward no-bullshit moral lessons were solid guideposts for social action. He was, despite his financial transgressions, a very religious man and bound to God. He could recite the scriptures from memory. Counseling parishioners had been his forte.

RJ would still be the pastor at Faith Tarzana church in Southern California if his penchant for Indian gambling casinos hadn't tempted him to dip into the building funds. It's true that he nicked the church for a half-million, but those were only material goods and that was holy water under the bridge. He'd never be able to pay it back. His offer to assume pastoral duties without a salary was rejected. The church elders were more interested in revenge.

Just before the case went to the jury, RJ jumped bail. That's why the former preacher was hiding behind an alias in a trailer in godforsaken Punta Gringa. He was, he told himself, biding his days until God forgave him and called him to service once again.

The rumble of pickup trucks coming down the road brought RJ off the porch. Two vehicles pulled up behind Rose and Doc's house. The drivers went inside and returned with a table and two chairs. Thieves? Or maybe Rose's relatives from Arizona? RJ changed out of his robe and shuffled over to the truck.

The Acosta brothers from Playa Refugio, Chuchu and Luis, were carrying a mattress and box spring out the door. Doc's battered upright piano sat in the driveway, waiting to be loaded. RJ spoke in Spanish.

"Hey. Buenas dias, guys. Hey, Chuchu, what are you doing?"

"We have to clean out the house. The ejido said she isn't coming back."

"But this is all Rose and Doc's stuff. What are you going to do with it?"

"We were told to store it in the old shed behind the ejido office."

"I think you should stop. I'll go chat with Señora Gabriela about it."

"Okay, we can wait. But if you don't call in two hours, we're back to work."

Despite endless ministerial training in conflict resolution, RJ wanted to crack somebody's skull. He was steamed. The Acostas were desecrating the place. It was time to go to the village and confront the all-powerful Gabriela. He never liked to do this alone. The scorpion lady overwhelmed him.

RJ walked across the road and barged into Merc's shack. Shay was lolling in the bed. She looked surprised.

"RJ"

RJ took this in stride. "Shay. Morning. God loves you."

"RJ. Morning yourself. The great spirit—she loves us all."

"Merc around?"

"In back. In the shower I think."

RJ walked through the house and found a scrawny naked Merc standing outside in the roofless back enclosure. Water was dribbling out of the showerhead protruding from a spider web of pipes hooked to overhead tanks and a burner.

Merc wiped the shampoo from his eyes. "RJ."

"Jesus loves you, Merc."

"I think he'll love me better when I'm clean. Did you get some coffee?"

"No, thanks. Had some." RJ went on to explain about the Acosta brothers taking stuff from Doc's house. Merc was livid. "Damn right I'll come with you."

When they reached town, Gabriela Cortez was sitting behind her desk at the ejido office.

RJ led off. "Jesus loves you."

Gabriela nodded. Merc did the talking. "Señora. Buenas dias."

"And good day to you. So, why are you ratas in my office?"

"The Acostas are on the sandspit looting Rose and Doc's house."

Gaby's face hardened. "Looting. We aren't looting it. Rose said she wasn't coming back, so we will store all this stuff for the family, if the family wants it."

"But you know and I know that anything in the shed gets stolen in Refugio."

"We added a new bolt and lock. It should be okay."

"Come on, Señora, you know that won't work."

"Yes, Merc, people steal things here. We live in the wilderness. That's the best we can do. If we catch someone taking things, we will deal with it."

Merc nodded to the carton of baseball bats stored in the corner. "With the bats?"

"We have no police. You know this method teaches them a very real lesson, yes."

"Can't you wait at least a few days? You people in the ejido shoved that battery plant down our throats. Couldn't put it out by the highway or in the village. You fucked with our health and now you are taking our furniture and our buildings."

"Don't yell at me. You are foreigners. I was born here and will live here as long as I run the ejido. The battery plant gives us thirty jobs. That money stays in this village and pays for the elementary school. Or for the children to go to secondaria in San Felipe. You guys get those pension checks every month. Mexicans don't."

"Well, don't mess with our houses."

"Merc. You know the lease. You know your houses are sitting on our land and if we want the land back, the house comes with it. You all know that. But you know that as long as I have a say, the ejido will honor our commitments to you. It's just when they go empty, well, it seems like we should fix them up."

Merc sensed the confrontation was out of control. "Sorry. I'm still upset about Rose and Doc." He motioned for RJ to leave. "Can we wait a few days, until this settles a bit? I apologize."

"Well, okay. A few days."

"Thanks, Señora."

"By the way, Merc, with Doc gone, we need someone to fill in on the Flying Medics clinic this Sunday. I can take Saturday. Can you do the intake on Sunday?"

"Yeah, I was sort of planning to do that anyhow. I can also handle the cleanup and get the equipment and medicos back to the planes."

Gaby offered a subdued smile. "Honestly, Merc. You always surprise me. You are such a fucking hothead but really do have a good heart buried somewhere. You do, you know."

"Uh,...don't jump to conclusions, Señora. Remember, I am one of your ratas."

"Oh, I know you are and will always be."

Outside, a massive, turtle green Ford 350 Super Duty Diesel pickup with light bars, monstrous knobby tires and a chrome cattle guard blocked Merc's truck. Standing beside it was Taras Burbank, their vastly overweight neighbor, a seasonal Gringan now down for a couple of months and the only sandspit resident universally despised by gringos and Mexicans alike, the man derisively called Taras Blubber. He pointed to Merc's dented ancient Chevy.

"I just knew that dirty piece of shit pickup was going to be yours, Stiles."

"Hey. What's up, Taras? Can't find a place to park your rock crusher."

"This spot in front of your dipshit little weenie truck will do. Besides, that Mercury outboard you said you fixed is still running badly."

"Well, hey. I told you it was never going to run right unless you took it to Arizona and got a fuel line specialist to fix your leak."

"I paid you to fix it, goddamit, and you didn't."

"You paid me to try to fix it. I told you that the problem was fuel starvation and I couldn't fix it here and you needed a big shop to do it."

"Well, I'm pissed off."

"Well, if you would listen, then you might get it running right again."

"By the way, have your seen that little twat Shay

around anywhere."

"That little what?"

"I need her to do some voodoo hocus-pocus on my Jordan. She has a jellyfish sting on her ankle."

"Shay's around Punta Gringa. Try her trailer."

"I don't believe in witch doctor crap but whatever cactus jelly cream she used sure helped my sweet Jordan. It's pathetic we all have to rely on that flake Shay. Now that Doc's a goner, there aren't real American doctors around. Mexico is so full of shit."

"Taras, this is the frontier. If you want doctors in shiny white coats, go to back to L.A. Now, can you move the monster truck so I can get out?"

"I'll think about it. By the way, I know ten year olds who could have fixed that outboard."

"Good. Take it to the ten-year-olds."

"Oh, and one last thing. I'm going to beat your ass in the Playa Refugio Fishing Challenge this year."

"Well. I don't know if I'm going to enter this year. It's a little soon after Doc's death."

"Yeah, use any excuse you want. Doc is history. Kaput. So it sounds like you know you will be a loser if you enter. I know a secret shoal that breeds fish."

"Taras, you're a dick."

Taras threw his cigar butt on the street and awkwardly hauled his portly body into the driver's seat of the most enormous off-road truck in Baja. He started the clattering diesel, revved it and blew a cloud of black smoke onto Merc and RJ. The he drove off, knocking over one of Playa Refugio's oil drum trash barrels.

RJ righted the trash container. Usually a gentle, soft-spoken man of God, he was blunt about Taras. "How did we get the world's biggest asshole as our neighbor?"

Merc shrugged. "Beats me. That guy has too much money. Did you know he used to work in the Hollywood movies? With explosives? Have you seen his 28-foot Albemarle cruiser? It's a beauty. Twin Merc 300's. Helluva boat. But he appears to be drunk most of the time. Goes fishing with his rifle and shoots at fish or anything on the water. What an asshole."

The pair headed back to Rose and Doc's place in Punta Gringa, intending to remove every last valuable object. On the way, they ran an inventory on Doc's guns. Shay had the .45 Colt and was keeping it. Merc had the modified assault rifle and a pistol. RJ said he still had one handgun.

But RJ had one more surprise. "I also found a bunch of papers. They might explain more about our mysterious friend Doc. I'll go through them and let you know."

"Some things," said Merc, "I'd rather not know."

9
Conflict

Castillo's drone Charley 2 had checked out three legitimate fishing boats, identified the crews, and logged their courses. Today's marine traffic on the open sea appeared as routine as his GrandeBurger lunches. This was frustrating. How was he going to improve his sagging bust totals if the bad guys were smuggling somewhere else.

Patrolling four miles offshore, he turned Charley 2 west and headed back toward the coast. Out of the blue, his Predator shook violently. There was a flash on his screen.

He opened the intercom. "Captain Dolan, here we go again."

Dolan hustled over. They replayed the video and this time, several frames showed an unrecognizable object maneuver below Charley 2. It was just a blur but both knew the flash wasn't something as innocuous as a sea gull. Not two miles up. Not at a hundred miles an hour.

"Okay, Castillo, you might have something there. I'm guessing that's the handiwork of our cartel friends," said the Captain. "Bring Charley 2 home on the double and have the maintenance boys standing by. They'll need to go over every inch of your drone. If there is so much as a scratch, I want the paint analyzed. Have all the electronics checked. Finally, prepare a frame-by-frame review from the nose camera. Maybe we can find a clue in the edge of the picture. And, cancel your plans for tonight. No one on Charley 2's team leaves today until we have answers. I want a post-mortem meeting once everything is checked."

—⚍—

In the cave, H contemplated his next move. His Courtesan intercept drone had performed perfectly this morning, sending out the Remora to make a tag with the three-inch disk. This was a dry run to simulate spoofing the Predator's electronics, when he could substitute his own control signals for the official ones, confusing the drone and allowing him to take control of the Border Protection drone and fly it to a hidden destination.

The attack today must have set off alarms. Within seconds after his Courtesan tagged the Predator, the Border Protection drone reversed direction, increased its speed, and reset its course to fly directly back to base in Arizona. H knew his Border Protection adversary—pilot Enrique Castillo—must have seen something.

The chess match with the Yuma boys was entering a new phase. It was time to uncork the defenses—misdirection strategies that would blunt the government's response, lead them in circles and lure them out to sea.

He powered down the communication gear in the cave. Then he sent out an untraceable signal to activate remote transmitters he had buried randomly in the seabed a year ago off of Puertecitos. Once set in motion, the tiny transmitters would emit signals that mimicked Predator drone control frequencies, but only for seconds at a time. They would alternate so a different duo sent the bogus signals each day.

If the guys in Yuma turned on their tracking equipment, they would be homing in on different offshore sources each day. The repeaters on the sea floor were set to pulse for only ten to twenty seconds, too little time for an aerial lock on. By the time a chase boat would finally reach the location, the transmitters would be silent. It would take scuba gear to find them. The phony signals were supposed to lead them to a phantom skiff on the water as the launching point for the Courtesans. He only hoped they wouldn't overreact and do something stupid.

But first, it was time to close up shop and go buy supplies. He had to prepare for a long stay in the cave, perhaps a month.

10

The *Jordanlovely*

Outside of Pepe the giant manta ray, Playa Refugio had little else to offer tourists. The two-block-long village was uninteresting. The two cafes were humdrum. There was only one motel and it had the concrete block charm of a school handball court. The silted up lagoon harbor was always bone dry at low tide.

Still, the ejido organized one semi-interesting yearly event. When its bustling northern neighbor San Felipe staged the annual Torneo de Pesca weekend fishing contest, Refugio unapologetically piggybacked on the publicity to sponsor its own low-key fishing festival—the Refugio Challenge. A mixture of local ex-pats and Refugian pangueros competed. The grand prize was an outboard overhaul at the Playa Refugio Motores Fuera de Borda.

This year the usual contestants from the nearby coastal settlements, still numb from the news of Doc's murder, sat out the Challenge. Of the twelve boats entered, only one came from the sandspit. That was the *Jordanlovely*, the 28-foot twin outboard cruiser owned by Taras and Jordan Burbank.

The Burbanks were determined to grab the trophy and show up their dismissive sandspit neighbors. They provisioned the cruiser with cases of Pacifico beer, stocked the bait well and brought along two high-tech fish finders. Setting out early on opening day, the *Jordanlovely* motored south to a shoal some four miles offshore of Puertecitos. This location had a history of bountiful catches.

Taras had a unique strategy for success. Once out of sight from the other contestants, he would tap into his film industry explosives experience and drop miniature depth charges that would stun the fish. The victims would float to the surface where Taras would put a hook into the mouth of the prizewinners. This would guarantee him a spot on the winner's platform.

Jordan Burbank had come to terms with her husband's unsporting approach. She parked herself atop a helm chair under the sunshade and concentrated on travel and leisure magazines while he drank beer after beer, threw the explosives overboard or shot the fish with his modified semi-automatic rifle.

Unknown to Taras and Jordan, their secret fishing spot was generating intense interest from a very concerned party. Charley 2, flying unusually low at only five thousand feet, briefly picked up the bogus drone control signal from one of H's seabed transmitters. Agent Castillo locked in on a 28-foot outboard cruiser four miles offshore of Puertecitos and dead in the water at the exact spot where the telemetry originated,

Enrique dropped Charley 2 down to get a better look. He reported seeing a fully dressed but petite woman on a helm chair, reading magazines, while a stocky, shirtless man stood aft. The man had a sizeable rifle and was apparently firing over the side into the water. Castillo was low enough to make out the cruiser's name—*Jordanlovely*.

On the boat, Jordan spotted the drone first. "Look at that honey, someone's model airplane."

Taras shaded his eyes with his hand. "No dear, that's some sort of drone. If that sonofabitch comes lower, I'll bet I can hit it. Don't get to shoot at planes much."

"Dear, don't do anything stupid. Why not keep shooting at the fish?"

"No worries. There's no pilot on board. It's a drone. I'll put a few holes in it."

Enrique watched dumbfounded as the overweight man pointed the rifle at the unarmed drone. On his monitor, Enrique was looking down the barrel of a gun. There were repeated muzzle flashes. He poured on the power and flew Charley 2 higher, climbing evasively until he was clearly out of range of the whacko rifleman.

Castillo called in the captain, who verified that a corpulent, shirtless gunman was firing from a pleasure boat, trying to hit a Customs and Border Protection drone. Dolan was excited. This might be a breakthrough in the crash of Charley 3. He'd get that pig with the popgun. They alerted a high-speed Mexican patrol craft stationed nearby off Puertecitos. The Mexican navy officer said his boat could get there in ten minutes.

Enrique continued to circle the boat. Meanwhile,

Dolan ran the name *Jordanlovely* through a Coast Guard database. This identified the owner as Taras Burbank, who lived in the San Fernando Valley in Southern California and who was a special effects demolition expert for the Cine Special Video production house.

Dolan concluded they were in a dangerous situation. He consulted with the Mexican counterparts, who authorized an escalated response to protect their sailors. The U.S. Air Force offered to divert a Reaper drone with Hellfire missiles to the location but the Mexicans said their aircraft would take care of the miscreant.

While Castillo kept tabs on the *Jordanlovely*, Taras kept firing. He paid no attention to the Mexican Marine's fast boat that came within a hundred yards of the port side of the *Jordanlovely*. The Mexican captain used a bull-horn to announce they were coming aboard. But Taras, six-sheets to the wind with a dozen beers under his belt, was intent on firing at the drone. He continued pumping bullets into the sky, missing the spycraft by a mile.

Jordan had trained her binoculars on the Mexican boat. "Taras. Taras, Honey. The Mexicans are putting on body armor. They look like they want to come visit."

Taras turned toward the Mexican boat. The Mexicans were serious about boarding the *Jordanlovely*. This led to another very bad decision. Taras fired several times in their direction.

Jordan was upset. "Honey, do you think that was wise?"

"Maybe not, but it's a beaner boat. Anyhow, I shot over their heads. Now they'll have to catch us. At best, they can only putt-putt along. Hell, I can outrun most anything." Taras started his twin Mercury 300 outboards and lit out full bore for the Playa Refugio harbor.

Taras miscalculated badly. With one outboard motor running rough, the Mexican boat was faster. It came alongside and fired a large caliber deck gun across his bow. Taras throttled back and hove to, settling dead in the water. A Mexican boarding party went onto the *Jordanlovely* and, as the entire Charley 2 team watched on the monitors in their Arizona trailer, the marines handcuffed the drunken Taras and the sober Jordan Burbank and wrestled them off the 28-foot Albemarle.

The grossly drunken fisherman was defiant. He got in the gunboat captain's face. "You Mexicans are hopeless. You've got to admit I almost outran you. But you are in for a big surprise. There's enough C-4 on my boat to blow all of Baja to Greece. I've got it rigged. If anybody searches it and opens the wrong door, they will be at the bottom of the Sea of Cortez. And I know what I am doing. So you'd better not touch it. Let's just tow it into Playa Refugio and call it a day."

The Mexican captain relayed the threat to his command.

But the handcuffed Taras couldn't shut up. He continued to taunt the Mexicans. "Hey pussies, why don't you guys go take a look. Yeah, board my boat. Fraid of a little bang-bang. You won't be dealing with some grade school pipe bomb."

That was enough. Both command groups agreed the *Jordanlovely* was dangerous.

The Mexican Marine commander called for air support. A military helicopter flew to the site and while the inebriated Taras watched from the deck of the Mexican fast boat, the Black Hawk let loose with a storm of M60 cannon fire. The fusillade struck the 28-foot cruiser in the wheelhouse and dispatched its fuel tanks, blowing up the expensive yacht. The Mexican sailors, glad they didn't have to board a ship with booby-traps, cheered as the hull rolled over and sank quickly. There were no secondary explosions.

Taras sat back, nearly catatonic. "The *Jordanlovely.* They sank my boat. I'll sue them."

Mexican federales met the fast boat in San Felipe and spirited its prisoners off to Mexicali, where Taras and Jordan were deposited in the maximum-security terrorist wing of the prison.

Very quickly, and after consulting the U.S Consulate, a Mexican court convicted Taras Burbank of weapons charges, resisting arrest, illegal explosives, shooting at Mexican police and being a generally obnoxious asshole. The judge sentenced him to three years in the Mexicali prison and, following that, immediate deportation to the U.S.

Jordan was released and made her way home to the San Fernando Valley. Both Burbanks swore they would never set foot on the sandspit again and their house, rumored to be booby-trapped with high explosives, became a derelict, empty and untouched. Even the vandals and thieves stayed clear.

When the story got out, the tabloids played it up. "Another Close Call with the Terrorists." "Suspicious Boat Rigged with Explosives Destroyed off the Baja Coastline." There were long stories about the apparent cooperation between both countries in snuffing the security threat and sidebar story about the U.S. spy drone involved in the incident.

But one headline, in the *LA Times*, foretold an onslaught of grief for the sandspitters. "Punta Gringa: A Baja Haven Gone Sour." When Merc read that online, he knew there would only be a few days to prepare for a new invasion of television satellite trucks and reporters.

It was time, Merc knew, to gather the Supreme Council of the Sandspit, to plan a defense.

11

Back Again

"You're kidding."

"Not kidding. One thousand dollars per reporter, 500 extra if you want to bring the truck, and only one news crew per day on the sandspit," said Merc, who was wearing an electric blue Speedo swim suit, boots, a Halloween chicken mask and a wide brimmed straw hat. He was standing in front of a hastily erected barricade of dead seagulls, Christmas tinsel and cactus husks at the top of the grade. A sign read "Private. Only residents and ejido officials allowed during festival week."

The cameraman driving the monstrous network satellite truck turned to the producer in the jump seat. "This is bullshit. Why don't I just drive through this crap and we can get on with the story."

"No. Last time...you remember the drone crash... the nutcases here refused to say anything, threw eggs at us and left dead seagulls in the satellite dish. It cost a fortune to clean it up. Let me try talking to this buffoon."

The producer rolled down the window. "You. You in the chicken mask."

"Yes?"

"When did all this gated community bullshit start."

"The Punta Gringa Supreme Council voted to restrict admittance and charge these fees during our festival week."

"Look. All we want to do is drive in for a few minutes, get some pictures of the crazy bomber's house and interview a few of the neighbors. What's the harm in that?"

"Interviews are 200 dollars each."

"You can't charge us for interviews. This is news."

"Take it or leave it. You might want to talk to your buddies in the four trucks in line behind you. Maybe you guys can pool your money."

"Can I ask what the masks are for? What the hell festival is it, anyhow?"

"It's the feast of St. Patchouli. For the next week, everyone in Punta Gringa will be wearing masks. We have cultural ceremonies at night, but you can't stay for those."

"This is loony," said the producer. "Look. We drove a long way down here. Don't you want to get your story out to the world."

"No. Not really. We don't want our story out. Or what you think our story is. We don't want you here at all. Now, I've got some things to do. Talk it over with your friends. I'll be back in an hour."

Merc drove down the hill to Eliot's driveway, needing a jolt of java to kick-start the day. Only eight o'clock but the June heat already radiated in waves off the sandy road and the thermometer was heading toward unbearable.

Everyone in the newly formed Supreme Council had agreed to meet for coffee on Eliot's patio.

Eliot was outside, in a tattered AC/DC tee-shirt, swim trunks and flip-flops. Unusually skinny, thirtyish, clean-shaven but with long, stringy hair, he was among the youngest of the *ratas*. He sat at a weather-beaten, wooden table. A light sea breeze rustled the palm frond palapa above his head. "Morning Merc. Coffee's inside. How'd it go?"

"The newsies are upset. I told them to talk it over and I'd be back in an hour. Anyone else here?"

"Not yet." Eliot grinned. "You know, Merc, I was thinking this would be a good time to poke around Burbank's house. I've always wanted plastic explosives."

"Eliot, you're nuts. I hope you're kidding, of course. But if you go exploring that place, please remember me in your will. I want your cow skull collection."

"If I go up in smoke, I would want you, and only you, Merc, to have the skulls. That's how much we are friends."

Eliot was an odd bird. His homemade shack was hidden behind overgrown plants, old outboard motor carcasses and cattle skulls he found in the desert. In the back, next to the palapa sunshade and outdoor shower, Eliot had installed an awning he scavenged from a restaurant in Arizona. The faded words "Caffe For All Seasons" welcomed visitors to Eliot's patio.

He was an on-again, off-again sandspitter, here for a week and then gone for three, following his compulsive passion for hunting fossils, exploring mines, scavenging artifacts, or dragging back any derelict bone, skull, or junk he found by the roadside.

Merc found it tricky to pry any information out of him. Eliot's obsessive purpose in life seemed to be staying anonymous in Baja. There were suspicions he had made significant money in the tech world. Others claimed he once told them he was a fugitive. Everyone knew he could troubleshoot any computer, work on most boat engines and patch fiberglass until you couldn't tell it from the original. Still, nobody knew Eliot's real first or last name or where he came from. He kept that info to himself and made sure it stayed that way. Eliot—just Eliot—was how he introduced himself.

Shay wandered in next. Still groggy, she went inside, returned with a mug of coffee, and plopped down in an old recliner under the palapa. Her trademark black baseball cap was pulled low. If anyone benefitted from Eliot's peripatetic lifestyle, it was Shay. She housesat for him while he was gone, watering his plants and sleeping or entertaining in his big, comfortable bed.

Merc nodded. "Hey Shay."

"Hey, kiddo? Where's everyone else?"

"They'll be here."

"Saw your latest blog. Says you'll be doing video. Really. Video?"

Merc pulled out a miniature white plastic camera. "Check this. I got this one button camcorder from the Acosta brothers. It takes that hi-def stuff."

Shay held the camera up to her eye. "Hope it works better than the fish finder that went kablooey? Hey. Ismael also told me Padre Nacho's in a bad way."

"What happened?"

"He was out in the desert searching for a missing kid from a ranchito when a rattler bit him. They didn't find him for four hours."

"I hope he'll be all right."

"They don't know. They gave him the anti-venom shot but he is pretty torn up."

Merc was surprised. "If I prayed, I would pray for him. He's a good man. Hope he gets well." Merc still was without coffee. He threaded his way through the scavenged debris in Eliot's front room, heading for the microscopic kitchen. That tiny alcove always spooked him, its walls covered by animal skulls and bones. But it was the place to score a mug of coffee. Back outside, he sat down next to Eliot, who was tinkering with a pile of small electric motors and model helicopters.

"Eliot. You're back with us again?" said Merc.

"I was in Southern Arizona looking for that abandoned McGill mine. Supposed to be salvageable ore. And unusual German mining equipment. But I couldn't find shit. The place had either been picked clean or the guy who sold me the map was running a scam."

Merc pointed to the helicopters. "Were those Doc's?" he asked.

"Yeah. I snatched them from the false wall in his place. These are interesting little models. I think there is more to Doc than we know. Maybe that's why he bought the farm."

"So what are you doing with them? Do they fly?"

"Well, I'll try to fly them. I used to build model planes when I was a kid. But these copters are weird. I think they communicate with each other."

"Bullshit."

"No, I mean it. Watch the red one. I start it and the others start buzzing. When I fly it, the other two will take off and fly with it. Like Canadian geese."

"You are nuts."

"No. I swear it. Remember, the red one is the mother ship. I'll start it up." Eliot pushed a button on the remote control and the rotor buzzed faster and faster until the tiny helicopter started hovering. "Now watch as it gets the others started."

He used the controller to steer the helicopter around the patio under the palapa. The other two tiny helicopters started up, rose off the table and joined it, slowly hovering together as a fleet.

"Now watch, as I go toward the house. The mother helicopter senses the outside wall and stops. The others won't fly near it. I swear to god, Merc, these things are communicating with the others. One tells another to avoid the same problem."

Just then, the following copters smacked into each other. One fell onto the stone floor, the other hit Shay in the head.

"Hey. Watch it."

"Sorry, Shay," said Eliot.

RJ arrived. He was still pulling on a ragged tee-shirt. His long scraggly beard and unkempt hair looked particularly wild. He was carrying his mask.

"Hey. Morning guys. Jesus loves all of us. Any coffee?"

"You know where it is. Grab a cup. Get one for Jesus, too. What's new?"

"Got out of bed this morning. That's what's new," RJ said. "Every day I get out of bed is a God-given blessing. Says so in Leviticus. Anybody want anything?"

"No. We're good," said Eliot.

RJ disappeared into Eliot's house and reappeared with coffee and two oatmeal cookies. He sat sideways in the hammock that was a perpetual fixture under the palapa.

"Merc. Did you do the news guys up on the grade?"

"I did. They aren't very delighted with the new rules. I told them it was the decision of the Supreme Council of Punta Gringa."

"Supreme Council. That's great. Do we have to wear these silly masks all day?"

"Only if the news guys decide to pay to play. And RJ, I was meaning to ask. Did you find out any more about Doc when you cleaned out his house?"

"I found a bunch of prescriptions written in Spanish. For large quantities of ephedrine."

"That's what they use to make speed. Why would Doc want speed?"

"I think he was paying back the Cubans," said RJ

"I had heard something about Cubans," said Merc. "Why the Cubans?"

RJ went on. "Doc told me he had a history with the Cubans. It started when Rose found out she had throat cancer. She and Doc tried to get her treated in the U.S. but the insurance companies said no because they weren't officially married. The Vets Administration turned him down too. And they wouldn't treat her in Mexico, because she didn't have any immigration status, only a long-term visiting visa."

"And…" said Eliot.

"And so Doc made this deal with the Cubans for Rose to get treated in Havana last year. It was long and painful but the cancer was apparently is in remission," said RJ.

"Do you think the Cubans were leaning on him for something?"

"I bet they were. His U.S. medical license would allow him to buy ephedrine without restrictions."

"God damn Doc. He never thought this shit through," said Merc. "Now it's the Cubans. And after the drone dropped out of the sky, I told him to shut up. No, he had to keep mouthing off."

"So. What are we going to do about this?" asked RJ

"Nothing. There are too many agents showing up in Playa Refugio. So, we keep our mouths shut. Stay out of it."

Shay put down her book. "I second that."

"Yeah. No one says anything about anyone," said Merc.

Eliot put the prescriptions back in a box with the helicopters. "Okay, I'm going to hide those notes. We'll just have to see how it plays out."

Ruby shuffled in. She was wearing a black tank suit and her chicken mask and carrying a long, macramé hanging interwoven with bird bones. "Hey guys. This is my newest one."

"I like it," said RJ.

"And I like our mask outfits. Merc, did you really tell them it's the feast of St. Patchouli?"

"I did."

"And what did they say?"

"They're thinking about it."

Merc waited until Ruby had some coffee. Three

more sandspitters, a Canadian couple that lived toward the south, and a retired teacher from Sacramento joined the group. They carried coffee cups and stood off to the side.

"Okay. Most everyone is here. I'm going back up. If they agree to pay, we'll have one crew down here for an hour. No one is to throw eggs or dead seagulls at them. You have to wear your masks, swimsuits, and if they interview you, it's 200 bucks. But you tell them nothing."

"How so?" asked Ruby. "What if they want to know about Burbank and his exploding boat?"

"Just tell them he kept to himself. Say he was a jerk."

"What if they ask about anything else?"

"Nothing. Nothing about drones, about Doc, about drug agents. Or about anything we've talked about last night or this morning. Nothing. Everyone agreed."

The crowd mumbled yes.

"So the goal is to let this die off of its own accord," said Merc.

Merc put his mask on and headed back up the grade. The road was empty and there was a note on the barricade. "Hey Chicken Mask. You can take your new fees and shove them. We shot some video of his house from here and we can get interviews we need for free in Playa Refugio. They appreciate news people there. You'll never see us again."

Merc smiled. That's what he wanted to hear.

12

The Clinic

The Flying Medics' light planes came in low over the western mountains and buzzed the Playa Refugio village, alerting a truck convoy it was time to head out to the desolate San Marcos airstrip. Two doctors, seven nurses and medical supplies needed rides to the El Parador Motel and Eco-Camp. The volunteers were on their biannual visit to provide free dental checkups, eye exams and care for minor physical ailments.

Merc could see black wreaths painted on the fuselages. Doc's name was prominent underneath, along with the words "Rest in Peace." The Flying Medics northern organizer, Dr. Saul Rosecrans, climbed off the wing and gave Merc a bear hug. "So sorry about Doc. Man, we are devastated. We heard it was a holdup or carjacking."

"That's what the federales say."

"It crushed us. You know he was in on the Flying Medics at the beginning. Now, man, he's gone."

"We can't believe it here, either."

"We want to hold a memorial moment to remember him at the Saturday night dinner. Also, we really appreciate your stepping in to help at the last second."

"I'm doing this with Señora Gabriela." Merc was getting emotional so he changed the subject. "Looks like you've got your full squad here. Where's Dave? I've been waiting for the Saturday night poker game."

"The game is still on but Dave couldn't make this trip. He's off flying some contract assignment. Charley filled in. And Merc, I hear you guys have a nutty manta ray. It's been all over television. I'd love to see the little beast."

"Pepe's not so little. If the tide's in, I'll take you out on Saturday afternoon. By the way, I was pushing the Mexicans to send a guy to do another evaluation on the battery plant. Did you pick up anyone in Ensenada?"

"I'll see if anyone knows." He turned toward an athletic woman wearing jeans, ankle boots, dark reflective aviator glasses and a red polo shirt with the logo for PROFEPA, the national Mexican prosecutor's office for environmental abuses.

"Veronica, this guy wants to meet the guy who will be doing the environmental screening."

"Really." Veronica didn't smile at all. She held out her hand. "Mucho gusto."

"Merc, this is the guy. Veronica Cruz. For the last 20 years, she has been the expert in detection of airborne pollution for the Mexican government."

Merc looked her up and down before shaking her hand. "Sorry. Mucho gusto."

"The same. So...the famous Merc." Veronica lightened up a bit. "You've been bugging our offices for three years about the battery factory. I expected you'd be some wild-eyed goofy old geezer."

"Sorry to disappoint. I expected you to be a guy."

"Maybe you don't believe a Mexican woman can do this job."

"Oh, I'm sure you are up to it. I respect Mexican women."

"We'll see about that." Veronica kept loading equipment into a truck. "So it doesn't sound like you believe our earlier tests that show no pollution."

"Oh I believe those. But I want to be sure that the plant stays clean."

"And that's why you keep emailing us. You have too many anxieties. That's easy to see from your blog."

"You've read my blog?"

"Of course. Everyone in the PROFEPA office enjoys your sarcasm. And your jokes. We all get a good laugh. And now I see you're going to do video. You have really been pissing off the Bat-Mex managers lately. They complain all the time."

"Yes, but I only report what I find."

"Well, I'll be doing the plant's official assessment tomorrow."

"Good. If you don't mind, I'd like come along, I can give you a ride."

"I'll be ready 9:30. But I'll be doing the interviews in Spanish. And like most gringos, you probably can't speak our language."

"I do. No problem."

Merc began loading equipment cases and Shay ambled over to help. "Hey, Kiddo, this Flying Docs event could be a cool deal. That pilot who replaced your poker buddy is Charley. From Utah. I'll ride with him to the El Parador."

Merc grinned. "Charley must be all of twenty-five. Your daughter's age. Are you sure you're able to keep up with such a stud muffin?"

"Why, Merc. Do I detect some jealousy?"

"No. Just didn't want to have to drive your exhausted body up to emergency in San Felipe."

Shay's eyes lit up. "Well, he has to work at the clinic so he doesn't have much time. Saturday night is free so I thought I could show him our jumpy manta ray. We can sit on the beach and watch Pepe breach in ecstasy."

"The ecstasy might be in your moldy trailer on the sandspit."

"Right, Kiddo. Actually, Eliot took off this morning for another freaky mine in New Mexico. I can use his place."

"Okay, Shay. I'd better bring over the scuba tank. You might need the oxygen?"

"Speak for yourself, old man. It's not often we get fresh action in here. How about you? I saw the pollution checker. I saw you eyeball her."

"Shay. Shay. A professional Mexican woman with a superior attitude is not my idea of a good time."

"Right. Don't tell me the possibility of passion didn't cross your mind. If things turn out differently, maybe we'll be sharing breakfast rolls under your palapa on Sunday morning."

"Whatever. Good luck with your boy toy Charley."

13

Veronica Warms

Veronica Cruz struggled with a bulky backpack and a cylindrical air-sampling wand fitted into a holster attached to her belt. She huddled in the shade of the vacancy sign at the El Parador parking lot but even in her shorts and tee-shirt, she was still soaked in sweat.

Merc drove up. "You're going to need a hat."

"No, I like the sun. I grew up in a place hotter than this."

"I've got an old one behind the seat and…"

"That's okay. Thanks anyway." Veronica jumped in.

On the way to the plant, Merc banged through every pothole on the unpaved road. Veronica's forehead smacked the pickup's headliner a couple of times. "You know, the trucks are always losing batteries when they drive on this crappy road."

"I will lose my temper if you keep deliberately aiming for the potholes. Please stop it. I get the point."

Manager Francisco Arcangel was waiting at the

gates. He smiled brightly.

"Well, I was right. Veronica. It is good to see you again."

"You too, Francisco. It's been ten years or so, hasn't it?"

Arcangel nodded in Merc's direction and he nodded back.

Veronica turned to Merc. "I knew Francisco from years ago. We both went to university in Mexico City. I saw the name, I thought—wow. I hoped it might be him."

Great, Merc thought. *These two are old buddies. That's not a confidence builder.*

"So, Dr. Cruz, officially, welcome to Bat-Mex. You may inspect anything you want. According to company policy, I must accompany you." He handed Merc and Veronica bright yellow hardhats with a Bat-Mex lightning bolt logo, disposable paper coveralls, and a respirator to cover their mouths. "You've got to wear these inside the plant."

Everyone donned the stuffy protective gear and the trio, resembling corporate astronauts on an expedition to an alien planet, walked awkwardly into a cavernous room where thousands of spent auto batteries were stored. From there, they followed a worker with a forklift, also wearing the protective clothing, to a processing floor where the plastic shells of the batteries were removed, the acid drained into tanks, and the lead separated out into bins. Those bins were then sealed and shipped by truck to Ensenada, where the lead would be loaded onto freighters bound for Chinese ports.

Veronica took samples of the air and wiped dust onto

swabs that she sealed into test tubes. She climbed up to check the exhaust ducts from the processing floor, as well as testing the interior storage shelves.

Back outside, the three stripped off the protective suits and Francisco passed out bottles of water. They rested in the shade before riding in an air-conditioned van around the plant's perimeter. Veronica was near heat-stroke but still had them stop three times to bag more samples. "I have to stop," she said. "I'm dizzy. It's just too hot."

It was almost two in the afternoon. Veronica gave Francisco a hug and the pair drove off in Merc's pickup.

"So what do you think?" Merc said.

"I almost died in that suit. I need something cold and I need it fast."

Merc handed her a bottle of water that was in the truck and she gulped it down. "No, I mean about today."

"It was good to see him. He was a lot of fun at the university."

"No, I mean the plant."

"Well, from all appearances, this is the cleanest battery recycling plant in all of Mexico or in the world. The workers are protected. They have high tech industrial scrubbers, the acid is controlled in redundant containment vessels and the lead is isolated until it is shipped. My serious concerns now are the trucks coming to the factory, especially if they hit all the potholes like you did earlier."

Merc ignored the sarcasm. "So you think it's really clean?"

"What can I say? It's got less pollution than a grocery

store. It's almost as if they aren't even processing batteries in this place."

The thermometer was 10 degrees over the century mark. The stifling heat had overwhelmed the ancient air conditioner inside the truck's cab. Veronica kept wiping the sweat from her face and neck. Merc was warming to the glistening sheen on her skin.

"You have a family?"

"A 17-year-old daughter at the university. And an ex-husband. How about you?"

"Just a string of ex-wives."

"No brothers or sisters?

"I had a brother but he died ten years ago. My parents are gone too.

"Sorry to hear that. Listen, at the Parador the first thing I'm doing is getting a cold drink. Join me? Or maybe we could go for a swim in the motel pool."

"Maybe another time. I've got to get back to Punta Gringa."

She thanked him for the ride and jumped out of the pickup. On the way back to Gringa, Merc regretted not taking up the offer for a swim. *Totally dumb. Then I could have brought her out here to see my place. Or Pepe. Why do I do this?*

Once home, he grabbed a cool drink and went out to his patio, relaxing in a hammock under the palapa. In the distance, Pepe was leaping and twisting offshore. The stark foothills to the south, usually chalk white in the morning sun, now glowed a cinnamon brown. This is a visual treat that Merc truly loved.

—ɯ—

The mood at the Saturday night dinner was subdued. Padre Nacho usually came to the free clinic to encourage the reluctant to get checkups. Now everyone was hearing about the tragic snakebite from Senora Gabriela.

"It is sad news. Doctors in Mexicali have said there is nothing more they can do for him. The snake venom went too deep into his system and weakened his heart. They expect him to die in a couple of days. I want you to bow your heads. We can all say a prayer for this great, unselfish man who did so much for our people. At the same time, let us also remember Doc. The village owes him too."

Merc sat with the flight crew during the meal. He stayed for ten hands at the poker table, losing two big pots. Veronica was also in the game, refreshed and clean in a stylish blouse and short leather skirt. She finished off a few margaritas and told raucous jokes while flirting with Francisco Arcangel. He kept putting his hand on her thigh and she kept pushing it off.

Their chumminess dismayed Merc. Sensing he was a loser on every front, he cashed out and fled back to Gringa, where he tried to sleep through boisterous love-making yelps from Eliot's place.

Sunday morning, Merc was up before dawn, opening the school classrooms that housed the clinic. About fifty locals from the village and nearby ranchos had lined up outside, waiting for the start. Merc worked intake, referring patients to individual doctors or nurses. Some spoke a rough, broken Spanish and needed an interpreter.

In the afternoon, he drove the equipment to the airstrip. Veronica was there, chatting with the doctors. Merc watched her give a smothering embrace to Francisco. When she spied Merc, she straightened her shirt and walked over. Rivulets of sweat rolled down her brown forehead.

Merc was attracted to women who weathered the desert. Veronica's makeup job was for the city and wasn't coping. Her mascara was strung out down her cheeks. He reached out and politely shook her hand. "Thanks for coming, Veronica. But get yourself a hat next time."

"Merc, I'll let you know about any results as soon as I get them."

"Good."

Veronica smiled broadly. "Stay well. You know, Gabriela warned me about you. She said you were moody and annoying like a bulldog. But keep blogging away. If I ever have to come back, maybe you could take me out in your boat and get close and personal with your manta ray."

Merc envisioned getting close and personal with Veronica, not Pepe. "Okay, okay by me. If Pepe is still here."

They called her to get on the plane. "Vaya con Dios," he said.

Would Veronica ever return? Would she report any problems? Merc doubted it. This summed up his frustration with Mexican officials. No one ever found the pollution Merc knew in his heart had to be there.

All the volunteers watched the planes take off and climb in formation west toward the sunset. Merc was a bit envious. It must be the hangover from Doc's death.

This violent episode had stirred thoughts about leaving Punta Gringa. Had he played out his string here? Maybe four years was plenty. Maybe it was time to scram, to get back on his horse and blow this joint. But then, with no family, he really had nowhere to go.

14

Escalation

Five miles west of the San Felipe-Puertecitos highway, in the gritty Sal Si Puedes Canyon maze, H sat outside the cave under the palm covered palapa. He was building a new anti-Predator lookalike he called the Decoy. Although half the size of Charley 2, the new decoy could carry enough electronics to exactly mimic the responses agent pilots saw from their Predators.

The Decoy was crucial. It would allow his Courtesan, flying below it, to sneak in, spoof their systems and make off with Charley 2. Before the Decoy's first flight, however, he needed one more rehearsal with just a Courtesan and the three Remoras. He knew Border Protection was on edge, watching and ready to spring. If they closed in on him, he had an escape plan—he could crash his flock into the sea, destroying the evidence.

At noon, a beeping signal announced that a Border Protection Predator was coming south from Arizona. At ten thousand feet, it slowly began circling the harbor at

Puertecitos. H was curious. Are they looking for druggies or his offshore signal buoys? Or him? After twenty minutes, the Predator began following a fishing boat leaving the coast.

That's when his monitors spotted the heat signature from a second Predator's Rotax piston motor. The companion Predator was out there too. This was textbook bodyguarding—using Castillo's drone as a tease and a having the second drone shadowing it. He shut down the radar equipment and fired up his powerful laser visual monitors. These worked when he had line-of-sight to their drones. Now he could follow them without electronics. They would never find him.

For the rest of the afternoon, he kept track of the drones in the air. He watched them until he was certain both Predators had finished for the day and were headed back to Arizona. Then he lay down on the cot in the cave and opened a can of chili.

In the morning, the alarms went off signaling new drone patrols. Again, there were double signals. Both Border Protection Predators were up, flying in formation. H had to assume he was still the target.

At ten a.m., his random seabed transmitters once again fired automatically from offshore locations near Puertecitos and Playa Refugio. He watched as the Border Protection drones headed for his repeater beacon sites. On schedule, these weakened so fast that the drones would be tantalized but couldn't lock on. The drones began flying erratic circles over a fifty-mile area, half over the open sea and half over the coastal landscape of desert hills. He was satisfied that they were confused and he went back to work shaping the Decoy. Soon they would tire and head back to Yuma.

Thursday dawned brilliant. At 10:30, the Border Protection drone Charley 2 appeared on his monitoring systems, flying lazily along the coast. There was no sign of the bodyguard. When the Border Protection craft was two miles west of the shoreline, H dispatched the Courtesan complete with a trio of Remoras. The intercept was underway.

Once his Courtesan positioned itself in the blind spot above the much larger Predator, all three Remoras launched. They surrounded the Border Protection drone, and one deliberately flew in front of the Predator's nose camera before attaching itself. Another flew beneath its ground imaging surveillance camera and then attached its disk. The third did the same.

On cue, two Remoras disengaged their discs and fell toward the ground. The third lagged back and, before spinning away, left a permanent three-inch wide disc as a calling card.

Today's intercept worked like a charm. The Border Protection folks clearly understood that Charley 2 had a visitor, and immediately turned the drone back on a heading direct to Arizona.

H relaxed in the cave. The next move was theirs. They would analyze the hell out of the data and would dissect the small electronic disc he had attached to the Predator. He wondered how would this change their tactics? Would they bring in advanced drones, the Reapers or the Guardians? Would they get the air force involved, drafting their top drone pilots for this operation?

He was willing to let them stew for two weeks while he prepared for the ultimate move. He needed to test fly the Decoy and work out the kinks. On the day he was ready to take Charley 2 down, poor Enrique would be pushing a joystick two hundred miles away and flying the substitute drone. In the meantime, H had to play it cool. They would send agents looking for him in all the settlements along the coast. He had a plan for that too.

15

Drone Scientist

In Yuma, the Border Protection field office was crowded, busy. Tank Dolan had called in scientists from the drone's builder, FlyTomics, and the U.S. Air Force. A half-dozen aeronautical engineers with degrees from the finest universities mingled with veteran drone pilots. Castillo was the only Border Protection pilot invited. He lacked university engineering courses, having earned only a certificate in hospitality studies and a minor in golf science from Furnace Valley Community College. But he was the pilot with mission experience at the console during Charley 2's high altitude drone skirmishes.

Dolan opened the session. "As many of you know, we have been experiencing attacks from the cartel against our drones. These have been baffling. Yesterday in the skies over Mexico it happened again but this time, they may have made a big mistake."

"Everyone. We have slow-motion playbacks from the cameras on Charley 2 showing two enemy craft, no bigger than three meters across. They flew through the soft focus in front of the cameras' lenses." The engineers watched as the drone monitors shook when several tags hammered against the predator's skin.

"The entire attack was over in seconds. The telemetry readouts from Charley 2 faltered for several seconds, but rebooted to normal when the tech crew in the Yuma office switched to a little used military satellite channel. Once again, it was clear the intercept signals had come from offshore sources, probably skiffs floating in the Sea of Cortez, but they had faded quickly once the attackers closed in on our Predator."

"The major surprise was the small metal circuit board disc that the maintenance crews found on Charley 2 back in Yuma. It was three inches across, affixed to the Predator fuselage near the wing root."

"So. What were the attackers up to? What was the significance of the small disc? Was it a botched attempt to force it down? How did these drones get into position to attack Charley 2?" Dolan paused to survey the room. "And now, I want to introduce Miss Ellen Byrne from FlyTomics, the company who builds our Predators. She's the lead scientist on drone air security."

Ellen Bryne strode to the microphone. Tall, rangy with broad shoulders, she wore her short brown hair in a shaggy cut. Her long face was pale behind thick, green tinted glasses. She was the only woman among the 20 men in the room. And she wasn't offering congratulations.

"Yes, there has been an orchestrated attack on an unarmed early model Predator known as Charley 2. Small aircraft carried it out. They were drones. We don't know how they were controlled. We picked up some weak spotty offshore command signals, but it's unclear how they might have influenced the interaction between the attacking drones. As such, this leaves us with little to go on for a point of origin. There was no sign of land-based telemetry from anywhere between Puertecitos and Playa Refugio."

"We know at least two drones were involved in the attack. We think they are small and have a limited range and ceiling. They didn't try to shoot down the Predator but simply maneuvered around it. How they got there and kept pace with our Predator drone was a mystery."

Agent Castillo raised his hand. She nodded in his direction. "Should we analyze this encounter from an outside-the-box perspective? Perhaps the attacking drones did not rise from the land or sea, but perhaps from a piloted mothership craft flying above the Predator. I've always felt that we needed to look…"

Byrne interrupted, asking him to wait until she had finished summarizing the preliminary findings. "Even more surprising. The maintenance crew found a three-inch-diameter metal circular disc attached to the drone under the wing root and two other impact points where metal tags had been applied but fell off."

"The disc had parts with U.S., Mexican and Cuban markings, and a tiny transmitter that used a sim chip from an Asian cellphone system. The electronics in the chip seemed to communicate with our Predator's GPS navigation system, but in a very minimal way."

"So," Bryne concluded, "we cannot even guess why this disc ended up on our bird. We wish we knew more but we don't. We only know that the cartel is after us."

Agent Castillo raised his hand. Once again, she nodded in his direction.

"Why are we assuming it was the cartel? If it was from above, could it have been from other forces we don't understand?"

Byrne finally recognized him as the pilot Castillo. Dolan had briefed her on his bizarre theories. She paused for a dramatic moment. "Agent Castillo. No, the physical evidence and the small disc are from earthbound—and I emphasize that—earthbound sources." There was a communal chuckle at her answer.

Enrique was not deterred. "Okay. Suppose it's the cartel. If we didn't locate any unique control signals during the attack, does it make sense to blame the cartel? Does the cartel have an unknown proprietary comm channel? Maybe encrypted? Or perhaps these attacking drones had no connection with any ground stations. Maybe they were operating autonomously."

"God, I hope not," Byrne said. "You're right. The evidence of guidance telemetry is slim to none. Yet once the smaller craft had swarmed the Predator, they acted as if they were communicating. That would demonstrate artificial intelligence messaging—something we know as fleet learning. I'm not ready to grant that to any operators from a two-bit Mexican drug cartel, unless, of course, they imported foreign scientists. Whatever their strategy, we'll know more when Langley analyzes the disc."

Castillo continued. "The disc. The disc that we found." Castillo pointed to the photo of the small device. "Do you think it accidentally stuck to Charley 2 or do you think these unknown forces wanted us to find this? To communicate with us? Or to confuse us."

This time Ellen Bryne rolled her eyes. She was tired. "Agent Castillo. It is a valid to ask if the perps wanted us to find the disc. But communicate with us? That is way over the top. This was no close encounter. I hear they call you E.T. Castillo. What happened at ten thousand feet was no outer space rendezvous. It's earthbound. As you reported several times in the past, they had apparently tried to attach a tag like this to Charley 2. This time, one stuck. I'm confident they didn't think we'd ever find this."

"What do you think our next step should be?" asked Castillo.

Bryne responded. "Supervisor Dolan has that information."

Tank Dolan picked up the thread. "The cartel thinks they are running this little game but we are ready to show them who's got the upper hand. We are getting two additional drones to attack this problem. They are the larger, more advanced MQ-9 Reapers that fly higher and use sophisticated capabilities to intercept communications. They will bodyguard our Charley drones from above and visually record any interactions. Air force crews will operate these craft from Creech Air Force Base in Nevada."

"In the meantime, we will swarm the beachside communities from Puertecitos to San Felipe with Mexican anti-drug squads to check on any type of communication gear along the coast. If anyone's house, shack, casita, lean-to garage, rust-flecked travel trailer, pickup truck, mobile home, shed, pasta colander, hot tub or even outhouse has a dish or antenna, we are going to check it out. Maybe these undercover operatives can dig up some clues. We will also focus on a smaller area surrounding the crash site of Charley 3."

Castillo groaned. He wasn't sure that harassing the isolated communities with agents was a good tactic. "Sir, there's a problem with that. How do we...?"

Dolan cut him off. "Castillo. Quiet for goddsakes. We already have our own agents checking out the population down there. Right now, our best guess is that the local Equipo 30 drug cartel is behind this. They operate along the 30th parallel across all of Baja. Our Mexican counterparts are preparing a major search for their hideouts east of Ensenada and outside of Mexicali. The joint operation forces will come down on them with the hammer."

"We also have intel that a Cuban agent is operating in the area. Perhaps the Cubans are using our Border Protection drones as field tests for their own anti-drone systems. We need to find these jokers. It wouldn't be the first time a government has hooked up with narcotics traffickers for political gain. Hell, we did that ourselves in our covert war in Nicaragua back in the seventies and the eighties."

"Whatever is going on," Dolan added with certain emphasis, "I guarantee the we are going to find who is fucking with our drones. And when we do, we'll wreak havoc on them."

16
Assignment to Hell

"Agent Castillo. My office."

Enrique had been sitting at his desk, catching up on his favorite Internet drone blogs. Now, something important was in the works. Dolan only addressed him formally when a critical official action was coming. Otherwise, it was just Castillo or Enrique.

Maybe he'd train to fly the advanced Reapers while they went after the cartel drone attackers. Or maybe he'd be the liaison agent with the air force pilots in the Nevada command center. That would be exciting.

"Close the door," said the Captain. He was holding up the local newspaper. "Enrique, do you read the *Yuma Sun*?"

"No sir."

"Then you probably don't know about this article." Dolan threw him the paper. The headline read "Strange Forces Attacking Drones from Yuma." The subhead was "Some Say It's Aliens".

Castillo scanned the item. It reported one drone pilot, who was not identified, complained that other-worldly forces were attacking his aircraft. "Whoa. Captain. I don't know anything about it. Where did they get this bullshit?"

"It says an unnamed source. Are you the unnamed source?"

"No sir. I've never talked to anyone about what I do."

"Are you sure you haven't mentioned this at the gym? Or at that sleazy fast food hamburger place…what is it… Lorena's Burger Adobe? Or could this have come from your old girlfriend Sylvia?"

Castillo looked at the article. There were things only he, or his crew on the flight line, or Sylvia would know. "Captain, it could have been anyone in this office."

"Okay, Castillo, I believe you. I didn't think that you would stoop this low. Anyhow, everyone is pretty jumpy after that drunken American fisherman's yacht was shot up. So now there's a new operation. We are going all out to get these crazies attacking Charley 2. As you heard at the post mortem the other day, we suspect it might be the Cubans working with the Equipo 30 cartel. They might be using inflatable boats anchored offshore to direct the drones. I wish the Equipo boys were more like the other, straightforward drug cartels. You know, just gang-bang violence. No, they've got to do things differently. They don't move coke. They hide in the hills. They fly drones."

"Yes, sir."

"Well, both FlyTomics and our agency want to get to the bottom of this latest scrape with those Equipo boys."

"Yes, sir."

"Border Protection and the Air Force are committed to this operation big time. You know they've allocated two high-powered MQ-9 Reapers for the mission. But here's the catch. While they are searching for the bad guys, the top brass is demanding experienced pilots at the Predator consoles. You only have had a few months flying these Charleys. The air force wants their pilots to fly both the Reapers and our Charleys. They'll go back to two-agent crews with an imaging officer at the second console. Both will operate out of the air base in Nevada. And we are going to send a liaison agent to work with them."

It would be a dream assignment. Enrique imagined himself at the air force base, strutting around in a flight suit and sitting in the officers' club, shooting the shit with the hottest drone flyers. At last, they would recognize his skills and not look down on him, as Dolan did, as some sort of glorified video gamer.

"I'm sending agent Hooper to Nevada to be our liaison with that operation. He's our most experienced pilot. That means I'm going to ask you to be a sport and stand down for a while."

Castillo almost choked on his coffee. *I'm going to be on the shelf.*

"But that doesn't mean you'll be sitting around here twiddling your thumbs." Tank Dolan paused for effect. "No, I've got a hazardous challenge in mind for you. Because of your father's expertise along the northern coast, and your 18 months in that area, I'm going to send you on a dangerous special assignment to the field to scrape up the leads and intel that will help us confront this drug gang. Your secondary objective, of course, is to find the drone attackers."

"Castillo, these are ferociously bad guys. The Equipo 30 cartel has a particularly unpredictable reputation. They don't go around doing mass killings or attacking civilians. But they are still lethal. You are going to be working solo. You may individually confront these jokers. If backup is needed, you can call on our toughest agents now working from San Felipe. It'll be mucho dangeroso, mucho, but we have to stop these crazy drone assaults at whatever the cost."

Castillo didn't know what to think. The Captain had smacked him in the head. No more leather chair and air-conditioned console job in Yuma. No, he was headed back to the dirty, dusty Baja desert to chase down a bunch of hardened criminals who would chop up their own mothers or barbecue their pets. And, lucky him, he would be the forefront leading the charge against these sociopaths. "Wow. I'm pleased you had the confidence in me, Sir."

"Well, we know you are a fine drone pilot but we also know you've been all over those back roads. I want you in the heat of it. Take chances. I want you especially to check out that joker named Doc who gave me a raft of shit when Charley 3 went down. I don't trust anyone who has such open hostility against the air force. Or drones. He lives on that shithole sandspit with those pathetic shiftless dropouts. No one who served honorably would be that antagonistic against drones."

"Okay, I'll do that."

"Castillo, I am supremely confident you will excel out in the twisted, desolate canyons where your father, the great agent..."

"Thanks, Captain."

"And you'll have a black Suburban four-wheeler with the tinted windows"

Castillo winced. *Oh, great,* he thought, *we might as well paint DRUG AGENTS on it. I could wear a black Tee-shirt with a giant DRUG AGENTS on it.*

"Sir, maybe this would be an op that could use an undercover car. Can we get an old beat up 4-runner or Pathfinder 4x4 confiscated in a bust out-of-state? Something they wouldn't recognize down there? Find something all clapped out but that runs well and doesn't look much like a department vehicle?"

"Good idea, Castillo. I'll have the boys in the shop get on that. We'll pop hidden radios in it. Anyhow, take the weekend off. You'll report to our safe house in San Felipe mid-week. We've got a room set up for you at our ops headquarters there. You'll work out of the San Felipe base and be staying until we nab these bastards."

"I should alert you too," the Captain said, "this could be a long assignment. So pack appropriately. You might be in the field for months. And, this being June, I guess you know it's going to get hotter there."

17

Heroes and Speed

Three or four days a year, gusty northerly winds rake across the Baja desert coastal plains, battering the populace with stinging sand-filled blasts. The pilots of Bat-Mex's twin-engine Cessna 404 air freighter were concerned. They faced a dangerous cross-wind takeoff on the short runway at the San Marcos airstrip. Today's cargo, specialized battery shells and processed rare metals, was both bulky and dense. The aircraft would be a tricky beast at low speeds. But they had to go now. They were due in Mexicali that afternoon. The pilots had made side deals.

On the run-up pad, the buffeting wind rocked the plane, slapping repeatedly against its right side. "This is pretty bad," the pilot said.

Finished with the preflight checklist, he pushed the throttles to maximum power and released the brakes. The heavily loaded Cessna lumbered down the runway, its right wing dipping down while it struggled for airspeed.

The worst was still to come. A powerful gust lifted debris from the nearby dumpsite and a swirling maelstrom of plastic bottles, paper bags, garbage and old car battery cases tumbled across the runway. The plane headed for the trash as the pilot struggled for control. The co-pilot yelled to abort but the pilot pressed ahead.

When he hauled back on the yoke, the plane lifted off through the rubbish storm. Shards of plastic whipped by the windscreen. Both pilots heard a loud bang.

"What the hell was that?"

The co-pilot looked over her shoulder. "Right engine is gone," she said.

An engine failure on this difficult takeoff was critical. The unstable plane was heading directly for the Playa Refugio village. The pilot muttered "we can't crash land it there," and began a dangerous low speed turn out over the Sea of Cortez.

But it was too late. The doomed air freighter quit flying about a half mile from shore off Punta Gringa. It entered a flat spin to the left, plummeting until it splashed down into water 100-feet deep. Although one wing snapped off, the fuselage remained intact and floated for enough time to allow the pilots to crawl free. Nearby pangueros sped to the crash site and pulled the pilots from the water. The rescuers had to restrain them from diving back for the plane. Then the wreckage slipped under and sank.

Merc and others in Playa Refugio had watched the plane falter and go into the drink. It was the second crash he had seen or been close to in the last month and he had had enough. He drove back home and sat on his patio, staring for hours at the afternoon light on the Sea of Cortez, not knowing that this tragedy was going to change many lives.

—∿∿—

The crash location became a sensation. Tourists, the townspeople and the locals crowded the beachfront near Punta Gringa to gawk at the salvage operations. Merc was there with his camera, making videos of the initial dive teams bringing up yellow debris bags and loading those into Bat-Mex pangas that sped away to a hidden dock. By the noon of the second day, two barges with cranes arrived from San Felipe and divers placed slings under the submerged wreckage and lifted it to the surface. On the first attempt, the fuselage broke in half and the cargo spilled out to the sea floor. On the second try, both halves of the crumpled plane were lifted onto a barge and then plopped down on a beach. The divers began bringing up the spilled cargo of precious metals and recycled battery cases.

Government teams were eager to examine the wreckage. Investigators from the federal Secretaria de Comunicaciones y Transportes, conspicuous in light blue jumpsuits, spent the day checking out the engine that had failed. Environmental scientists and divers probed for pollution that might have contaminated the sea bottom. Plainclothes narcotics agents in black shirts and jeans swarmed over the waterlogged skeleton, looking for obvious clues to smuggled drugs

Of more concern was Pepe, the manta ray and spectacular tourist draw for Playa Refugio. Since the crash, he had gone slightly berserk. As the beachfront crowds watched, he began a 24-hour period of continuous breaches, leaps and twirls. The 2,000-pound youngster was putting on the most astonishing aerial display anyone had seen.

Antonio the marine biologist was not pleased. "He's slightly crazy," he reported. "In the literature, there is no record of a giant manta doing this. I have no idea what is going on. It looks, and I hate to say it, like he is drunk. Borracho"

This posed a new danger. Pepe's most spectacular aerial gymnastics were coming perilously close to nearby tourist-laden kayaks. In one elaborate breach, he landed on three boats, swamping them. Others rescued the paddlers. The marine biologists immediately ordered everyone out of the water, until the agitated ray calmed down.

Antonio positioned two of his interns to watch Pepe's every move. They lost track of him. "We don't know where he is. He isn't breaching any more."

"Stay where you are. I'll get boats out there," said Antonio. But the search was fruitless.

The next morning, joggers spotted Pepe beached in the coastal shallows just south of Playa Refugio. Antonio rushed to the site. Pepe seemed to be breathing slowly and his eyes were dazed. Slack tide was coming in six hours and Pepe would be danger when the water levels were lower. Antonio and his assistants swam to him and took blood samples. They begged for help from the salvage crews at the plane crash site. The tugs pushed the cranes over to the beached manta and the biologists rigged a canvas cradle to lift him into a deeper lagoon.

Antonio conferred with manta specialists. "We all

concluded that he must have ingested a batch of contaminated plankton," he said. But the blood samples were negative for food poisoning. Instead, the samples revealed a startling concentration of something else—speed. It seems everyone's favorite manta ray was tanked up on crystal meth. Pepe must have fed on plankton near the crash site and now was loaded with amphetamines—the first recorded manta ray drug addict.

The media loved the story. Once again, the television crews and the news jackals flocked to Playa Refugio. The manta ray's dopey bloodshot eyes went viral across the Internet. "Big Ray on Drugs" "Devilfish O.D.s on Ice" "Stoned at Sea" were tabloid headlines that sold very well.

Antonio knew the next event might be a withdrawal episode in the shallow lagoon. And it happened. Pepe began thrashing and flapping his wings. He made a high screeching noise by rubbing together patches of his rough skin. The biologists brought out buckets of plankton from a clean source down the beachfront but Pepe wasn't eating. They gave him a sedative and once he calmed down, the townspeople and local children paddled kayaks out to his resting place. They formed a ring in the water where he lay. Padre Macho Nacho led prayers for their visitor. "Please. Do not take our friend who has delighted up for weeks. We have destroyed him with our weaknesses. Help him to get through this rough patch so the tourists can keep coming to see his exploits."

Pepe still showed no improvement. "I think we are losing him," said Antonio.

Finally, Gabriela made a last ditch effort and invited La Gringa to see if she could soothe Pepe. Antonio agreed immediately. "I have no other answers," he said.

La Gringa was delighted. She paddled out alone in a dingy, with a garland of flowers, strings of plastic manta rays she bought from the Acostas and a bucket of goat food. In the eerie quiet after dark, she played the guitar and sang lullabies to the distressed manta. She launched an armada of candles floating in small waxed cartons. La Gringa was on the water all night until the sun finally pushed above the horizon at daybreak, when she rowed back to the shore and disappeared.

The marine biologist did a quick check. "Another miracle," he said. "Pepe's still groggy but breathing more normally." At the moment the tide was highest, Pepe began shifting as if waking up from a coma. He thrashed a bit, flapped his gigantic wings and swam off. About a half mile offshore, he breached one last time and then continued south. He was never seen again.

Gaby had watched her exotic tourist attraction disappear into history. "Well, there goes our meal ticket. Off to rehab somewhere. It was great while it lasted. At least," she said, "we still have the tee-shirts, and his love and his story. We will keep our fiberglass replica out by the highway. I'm sad to see him go."

18

Springing the Trap

"We sicced the federales onto a big shipment today," agent Hooper reported. "The perps they nabbed were from the Ramos cartel."

Border Protection had turned over all drone flights to the Air Force in Nevada. Hooper had flown there to be the liaison and dutifully called every two hours with an update.

But the Captain was confused. "I don't understand. The Ramos cartel isn't even on our radar. They're from TJ. Why aren't we picking up the Equipo 30 guys? Why is Yuma the only Border Protection office pursuing an underperforming drug cartel that stays invisible?"

Anxiety was gnawing at Dolan. His career could soon be a shit sandwich. The two-year evaluation was coming. So far, his incompetent underlings had lost one four million dollar drone, provoked the Mexicans into rocketing a blowhard U.S. citizen's expensive fishing cruiser, and now requisitioned costly air force assets to frantically defend

another drone. One of his pilots had publically
announced they were under attack from outer space
aliens. Tank worried he might not make it to retirement
at the end of his stint with Border Protection. He'd be out
early on a miniscule pension that wouldn't be enough to
buy popsicles, let alone keep up payments on the beachfront condo he had picked up this month in San Diego.
Then again, if his agents could help the Mexicans stop
the Equipo 30 bad guys, perhaps all would be forgiven.

"Anything else?" Dolan asked.

"Yeah," said Hooper, "but I'm not sure what it is.
These guys play it super secret. They won't tell me but
they have something up their sleeve."

—⚏—

H was holed up in his cave waiting for a clean shot at a
Border Protection drone. He brought mystery paperbacks
and enough canned chili, water and beer to last him for a
while. Watching the Reapers trailing the Predators made
him uneasy; the game of cat and mouse was escalating
beyond his expertise and experience. The bigger, higher-
flying Reapers had come on-line after he left the agency.
With them dogging the Predators, he'd have to either
strike quickly to nab Charley 2 or spend more months
analyzing the Reaper's defenses.

And he was hoping for one more Remora practice
run, one more swarm, before he went after the Predator
with the newly built Decoy and the Courtesan mothership.

This morning showed promise. A solo Predator, one
of the Mexican anti-drug drones controlled from

Monterrey, was offshore of Puertecitos heading for the coast. It was in perfect position for an intercept.

Was this a trick? Did the Border Protection guys work with the Mexicans to set a trap? A ringer? If they did, it would have been a very unusual move.

With little time to find out, he moved into action. He readied the Courtesan and his last three Remoras. After confirming the sighting and locking on with the visual gear, he launched his mothership. Let's see now if everything is ready.

The Courtesan performed flawlessly, approaching the Mexican Predator and sliding into formation above it. The Remoras roared out on schedule, accelerating to position themselves next to the bigger drone. This worked like a charm. The Remoras attached their disc tags that set off their electronic dirty work. Now he was ready to rehearse spoofing the Predator. Then—disaster.

Alarms went off. The monitoring equipment lit up. Radar was bouncing off of every canyon wall. H had taken the bait and the spring slammed down. H had flown his Courtesan into a trap. The Mexican drone was itself a tactical decoy; his adversaries were watching very carefully. If he allowed the Courtesan and the Remoras to spoof the Predator and give away his capture plan, they would know his strategy.

He would have to sacrifice his handiwork. He pushed an abort button to emit a single pulse on a high-frequency radio band. The discs disengaged and fell off. The Courtesan and its Remoras turned abruptly and headed for waypoints out to sea. The drones would home in on the buried repeaters, and then plunge violently toward the salt water from two miles up. Hitting the Sea of Cortez in a 100-mile-an-hour dive would finish them off.

His heart was pounding. Damn it. The Air Force had bested him. Their subterfuge was incredibly sophisticated. Today was a major setback. He had been greedy. Now he'd have to start over building a second set of Courtesans and Remoras.

But he had planned for this. He was ready to manufacture new drones. It would take two days to complete the airframes and another two to stuff them with the electronics.

It had been a sobering encounter. He was happy to have escaped. His enemies were smart. This humiliating exercise would toughen him up for the big time.

19

Success

"Moscotrap. Moscotrap. Hey…Moscotrap." The air force drone pilots in Nevada were chanting, conga dancing and celebrating outside the base operations center. This followed a half-hour orgy of backslapping, knuckle bumping, high-fives and shit-eating grins inside the flight trailers. During the merriment, neglected drones on patrol wandered aimlessly around the skies over foreign lands. Bad guys strapped with bombs climbed into cars and got away. No one in Nevada noticed.

No, they were in full celebration mode. Their ambush op—officially called Moscotrap—had succeeded. Apparently, the drug cartel and the Cubans couldn't resist the bait and had lusted after the solitary Mexican drone. When the attackers went for the cheese, the air force MQ-9 Reaper drone flying a mile-and-a-half above it took revealing pictures of the entire episode. They now had the whole enchilada on slow-motion replay.

After five, the Moscotrap staff and pilots had gathered with pizzas and cold beer in the briefing room. Reps from FlyTomics had flown in once they heard the news. Air Force Base Commander Colonel Bob Perkins entered. Someone yelled "Attention."

"At ease. Great job, everyone. You deserve the beers. Let's get started." He gazed around the room and stopped at Ellen Byrne. She was biting her fingernails while poring over readouts and grainy still pictures and, as usual, looking less than satisfied. "Why not have the manufacturers begin. Everyone, Ms. Byrne from FlyTomics."

The usually pessimistic scientist had skipped the beers. "I know you guys are delighted that Moscotrap worked. But don't get cocky. We are up against very clever scientists working for the cartel. Our Reaper video shows they use a mothership drone that approaches our Predators in a blind spot, then releases its own fleet of smaller drones and, we assume, controls those drones while they swarm around."

"For us, this is unexpected. The blind spot approach. We have scant experience with counter-drones that use localized onboard artificial intelligence and swarming tactics. The attackers obviously have extensive knowledge of our drones and have clearly zeroed in on our weakest areas."

"We know the cartel drones are small, with a wingspan about three meters. They have delta wings, pusher props and electric motors. We guess they use a laser visual lock, not radar, to creep up on our birds. We don't know how fast they can fly or how far, or how long they can keep up with our drones. They are, if you will, almost like model airplanes with a very limited range."

"So although we do have an idea of the hardware they are using, we still are up against a big question mark. We also don't know where they come from, why they are up there...or what the hell they are planning to do."

"Clearly, if they can attach a small disc to one of our birds, they just as easily could have shot it down a long time ago. Instead, they let them slip away while they keep banging on our drones. So, why didn't they just knock our Predator out of the sky? What could they be looking for? They want something. We are guessing they may be using these Predators as laboratories, figuring out ways to spoof the systems."

"And another oddity. Once we sprang the trap, all the drone attackers headed out to sea. This may lead to a promising find. A local fisherman two miles offshore south of Puertecitos found fiberglass shards floating in the water. Our analysis showed that it is common nautical material and could have come from a boat or shoreside pier. But pieces of this particular fiberglass had been shaped into miniature curves. It also could have been the fuselage and tail fin from a drone. If their drones are all fiberglass, it would also show us a different radar signature."

Ellen Byrne was getting agitated. "My friends, they are clearly screwing with us. Gaming us. Harassing us. Making us waste a lot of effort, time and money chasing them. And maybe that's it. Remember what a magician does—misdirecting the audience to look somewhere else while she pulls the rabbit out the hat. Maybe this entire scenario is misdirection. Maybe while we spend millions screwing around countering their drones, the cartel is busy doing something else, something we aren't seeing.

We need to be smart about it. I would propose a tactical plan that responds to their drone harassment while, at the same time, seeks an answer to the larger questions."

She paused and changed the display screen to an image showing a conventional-looking missile mounted on a pod beneath the Reaper. "We badly want to capture one of their motherships. So, we will arm the bodyguard Reapers with something that is currently in development —a miniature Hellfire air-to-air missile called the Skyfire. These Skyfires were going to be countermeasures in Afghanistan but never got used. They can strike a small drone and disable its engine. The Mexican government and Mexican air force have approved our test use of these."

"Our role now, as I see it, is to bait them to go for the cheese again. If that happens, the Reaper flying above it will let go with the Skyfires. Then, hopefully, we can scoop up the parts and reverse engineer it."

"Questions?"

Hooper had raised his hand. "How can the Skyfires track a target without a metal structure? And, won't the explosions destroy the evidence?"

"The Skyfires acquire the target with an electronic lock-on but after that, must use visual aiming. We think there is a chance we can disable their mothership without blowing it to pieces but it hasn't been tried in action. We did tests against Raven drones and we had a sixty percent kill ratio. One or two targets hit the ground partially intact. Not great but better than nothing. So we'll have to see. But it is our only option, short of throwing a net over the attacker drone."

Agent Hooper was skeptical. "What if the Skyfire

misses and blows up Charley 2 instead?"

"This can be avoided. We have anti-lock-on proto-cols. Using these will prevent a slipup. We'll work out an ambush scenario that keeps our Predator out of harm's way. But if that doesn't work and we shoot down our own aircraft, probably all of us will soon be washing floors at the Thule Air Force Base in Greenland." This brought a groan from the audience.

"So, colleagues. We are moving into a brave new world. Drone to drone warfare. I know Coronel Perkins has been working on combat tactics. Coronel?"

Colonel Perkins rose. "Thank you, Ms. Byrne. We appreciate the analysis from FlyTomics. Our air force pilots will be rehearsing air-to-air scenarios in the simu-lators. Our pilots should stay after this discussion. For everyone else, thank you for coming. That's all."

20

In the Streets

The chaotic political rally underway in Refugio was the first ever in a village where six people sitting together at dinner constitutes an unruly crowd.

About fifty Mexican college students were in the street raising hell, chanting slogans while carrying enlarged photos of batteries on signs that said, "Close down the polluter" "Don't take the gringo's waste" and "Don't harm the manta rays." The students were from a private university in Mexicali, a school where Merc had guest lectured several weeks earlier on his crusade against the battery plant.

The protestors set up garbage can barriers at both ends of town. They spray-painted slogans on concrete block buildings and walls in the two-block long village. Crews from television stations in Mexicali, El Centro and Yuma were busy putting the demonstration on video or feeding it by satellite to their viewers. Isolated Playa Refugio was once again in the world's news spotlight.

Grim-faced local residents watched from vantage points along the main street. Two angry groups emerged from the Loncheria and began heated arguments with the demonstrators. Loud shouting surrounded the issue of jobs versus the environment, contentious topics that involved more pushing and shoving than polite conversation.

Merc drove around the end of the crowd and parked behind the El Parador. When he sat down at a sidewalk patio table for the morning coffee, he hoped for a bit of peace. But that would not happen. Amid the growing chaos in the streets, the students recognized him. A heavy-set and serious looking woman with glasses approached.

"Merc. Merc. Glad you could come to our demonstration."

"I didn't know anything about it."

"It was on Facebook."

"Well, I guess I missed that one."

"Anyhow, we are trying to get all the battery recycling plants closed, at least until the government sets realistic standards for pollution."

"I think that will be tricky. This is about people's paychecks. This stupid demonstration is only going to provoke the locals. And, you are defacing our village."

As a television crew approached to interview Merc, a pickup from the ejido office pulled up in the street. There were two men and a woman in the cab and six burly men in the back. Gabriela, with her black baseball cap and huge dark glasses, stepped from the truck and waded into the student demonstration. "Who is in charge?" she demanded.

A tall, broad-shouldered man with a shaved head, multiple earrings, and a long beard stepped up to her. "I am," he said.

"Well, you've had your say. You are painting graffiti all over our town. We'd like you to clean it off and stop messing with the people in our village."

"We want you to close the plant."

"There is little or no pollution from the plant. We need the jobs and we won't be closing the plant. You, however, are defacing our village with your graffiti and you'll clean it all off before you leave."

"We think you should reconsider."

"You are outsiders and we suggest you begin scrubbing off the walls."

"Are you threatening us?"

"Take it any way you want. This is our village and you are defacing it."

"We won't leave. You'll have to arrest us."

Gaby was direct. "Listen. We don't have any way to arrest you. There are no police here. We take care of criminals in a much simpler way. Either you start washing the walls or we will punish you unmercifully before we throw you out." She pointed back at the men in the truck. They carried baseball bats.

The imposing demonstrator turned to Merc, who had been sitting quietly at the table attempting to read his magazine. "You. Stiles. You came to our school and urged us to make noise. To fight pollution. Come out into the street with us."

"Don't drag me into this," said Merc.

Three ejido members moved to form a protective ring around Gaby. The burly protestor panicked and pushed his way out, shoving Gaby as he did. She fell against Merc's table, knocking over his coffee.

Merc did nothing. Then he stood up. "I'd better leave."

"That's right. Hit the road, gringo. Like you always do," she said and she picked herself up.

A scuffle broke out on the street by the Loncheria and the ejido enforcers ran off. More protestors came up onto the patio and the melee at Merc's table began again. This time Gaby found herself in the midst of an unfriendly crowd. Protestors bumped her and shoved her back and forth. Merc leapt from his chair and pushed his way into the mob. He reached Gaby and pulled her away.

Gaby was mad as hell. "Get your hands off me, Merc. Go on. Get out of here. I don't need your help."

A protestor on the veranda grabbed the back of Gaby's sweatshirt. Merc gripped him around the neck and wrestled him to the pavement.

"Hey, gringo, this isn't your fight," said the student.

"Yeah. It is now, pendejo. This violence is stupid. You are vandalizing our town."

"This is political speech, gringo."

"No, this is violence." Merc stood and picked up a baseball bat from the carton beside the truck. He raised it over his head, menacing three demonstrators.

Gaby stepped between Merc and the knot of protestors. "Back off, Merc." She was in no mood for compromise. She confronted the demonstration leader, who was brushing himself off. "Talk this over with your compatriots and get started washing the walls." And she forced him back off the patio.

The bedlam up the street had calmed. Their leaders called the students from the roadside to a meeting. The heated conversation went on for ten minutes while the ejido enforcers and locals watched. Finally, one protestor blew a whistle and they made a break for it, running chaotically for their cars. Before the bat-wielders from the ejido could react, the students were roaring out of town. Some in the crowd threw rocks. The ejido hit squad ran after them and smashed a few windshields but the protestors got away.

Merc remained at his table with the bat in his hand. He had never stood shoulder to shoulder with the Senora before.

She was stone-faced. "You. Picking up a bat. I figured you would just leave. But, no, instead you lose your composure. Such a hothead. I am astonished that you called Refugio our village. I suppose I should thank you, Mercury Stiles. One minute you speak at the university and that little lecture lures these vandals down here. Then you turn on them like a wild animal." She paused to rub her eyes. Merc noticed how weary she looked. "I don't understand you," Gaby said. "Now tell me, who will pay to clean this up?"

"Sorry. I just got carried away." He handed her the bat. "I didn't invite them. They came down here because of the battery plant. Make Francisco pay to clean this up."

"Merc, this is maddening. We've lost our meal ticket manta ray and now your students come down here to deface the town. This hurts."

"Gabriela, Pepe left because of smugglers. And these aren't my students. I never invited these jokers down here. Make Francisco pay."

"I will. But your little classroom pep rally up in Mexicali was reckless. It has really pissed me off." And she motioned for her ejido workers to meet with her on the main street.

Ismael brought out a second coffee and Merc sat for a long time at the El Parador. He was at a loss. His guest university appearance and his simple blog about the plant were now causing collateral damage. And Gabriela? In a vile mood. Time to be very careful. Stay out of her way. It was dangerous to offend this woman who controls so much. This might be another reason to flee.

21
Chasing the Devil

This piece of crap is so messed up, he thought, *it is perfect. This looks exactly like the scrap iron everyone else drives down there.*

The vehicle request came through. The Captain rummaged in the drug raid impounds in Colorado and found Castillo a clapped out Toyota 4-Runner 4x4 with oversized off road tires and a beat-up camouflage paint job. It had been jacked up for more ground clearance and had enough dents to call it corrugated. Bumper stickers extolled a Denver medical marijuana dispensary and the Broncos football team.

This was not how Enrique pictured his summer. He was headed across the border to San Felipe in June, a time when the northern Baja coast can be a suffocating vision of unbearable hell. And the gangs he would be chasing—well, they would be ruthless, violent and well armed.

On Tuesday, high clouds moved in and the temperature dropped. Enrique drove to the safe house in San Felipe, stowed his gear and wandered down to the *malecon*—the harbor seawall promenade. He planned to hang around and strike up conversations with the boat captains. For this bit of undercover work, he dressed like a tourist fisherman, decked out in an old tee-shirt from an Encinitas bait shop, jeans, fluorescent green tennis shoes and a San Diego Padres baseball cap worn backwards. He added a stage prop mustache and two wash-off skull tattoos.

A boat captain sitting on the rock wall untangling fishnets offered the traditional conversation starter along the malecon.

"Looking for a boat?"

"Not just yet. But how's the catch?"

"Not too bad. Cabrilla around here. Yellowtail to the south. I'll give you a deal."

"Maybe later. Had a lot of action with foreigners? Did you go out on manta ray excursions?"

The panguero eyed Castillo suspiciously. *He looks shifty. Could be another government agent.* "Si, the manta helped." And the panguero turned back to the nets.

Enrique was curious. This fisherman had clearly been spooked. He was way too cautious, unlike the usual hungry panguero eager to sell a boat ride. *"Buen dia—* good day" he said and moved on down the waterfront.

Before long, it was obvious the atmosphere was poisoned. Casual conversations at the outdoor sidewalk tables at Rositas and later on the veranda at the Bar Miramar next door confirmed this. Locals were nervous. They told stories of the so-called "hot" squad agents from both countries swarming the coastline, busting into trailers with satellite dishes and tearing up the furniture at gunpoint. *So stupid*, he thought. *This will make my job tougher. The drone attackers are smart enough not to leave mountains of evidence in any old rat-ass trailer along the shore. It will take a real agent to find it.*

The next day Enrique took his clapped out 4-Runner on a run south of San Felipe. At Playa Refugio, he bought a heavily discounted Pepe the manta ray tee-shirt from the Acosta grocery and ordered a diet soda at the Loncheria la Pasadita. Among his fellow customers at the ramshackle eatery, he recognized two undercover agents he knew personally. A threesome arrived later in a black Ford Crown Victoria with tinted windows. *What jerks*, he thought.

The waiter, knowing he wasn't a local, supplied him with an endless string of overpriced Coca Lites. Castillo had been trying to make eye contact with a dark-skinned gringa sitting alone at the next table. She was drinking a Pacifico beer and appeared to be engrossed in a book on a diet to treat anxiety.

She's hot. She might have some intel.

He turned to the thin woman with a black baseball cap and tattoos on her arms. "Excuse me, but I see you are reading Dr. Fleury. His ideas are terrific. I tried out his diet but couldn't stick to the food." And Enrique flashed his brightest, welcoming smile.

The ex-pat woman looked up. What did this grinning American jerk with the horrid mustache, half-assed tattoos and a manta ray tee-shirt want? What was he doing in Playa Refugio? "Yes, he's right on," said Shay, as she turned her attention back to the book.

"Hi. My name is Poncho Aguila. I'm from Colorado and I was looking for a place to kick back for a while." He stuck out his hand.

Shay ignored the outstretched palm. "Hi. Don't know of any places." *This guy is asking too many questions. Has to be a government agent...or just a creep.* And she put her nose back in the book.

Enrique bristled at her brush-off. Usually he got at least half a smile from the ladies when he hit on them. Maybe his prop mustache was crooked. Maybe, he thought, she made him as an agent. There might be too many competing anti-drug squads swarming over the place. Everyone who lived here seemed edgy, paranoid.

As an agent needing information, what would dad have done? What would El Toro's next step be? Enrique is the *aguila*—the eagle—and needs to soar on his own. He paid for six Coca Lites and walked up the street to the ejido office. He peered in, and entered.

"Buenas dias."

"Buenas dias," said Gabriela Cortez. She looked up —unsmiling.

"I'm thinking of spending a few months in an out of the way the place. I'm looking to rent a beachside trailer or casita in the area? I don't want to be bothered by people."

Gaby sized him up. "Stand still," she commanded. He did. She slowly walked around him once.

Hmmm. Young. About 28. Recent haircut. Pathetic gang tattoos. Mexican in appearance but speaking unaccented gringo Spanish. Wearing a bad false mustache. Has to be a drug agent. No sense getting mixed up with this guy.

I'll never rent to him.

Gaby switched to English. "Sorry, nothing now."

"Can you tell me if something is coming up? Can I get on a list?"

"Sorry. The waiting list already is long."

"Well. I'll check back with you. Maybe something will come up. My name is Poncho Aguila." Castillo wrote down his phone number and turned to leave.

"Wait," said Gaby. She knew she might regret this but she was still pissed at Merc. His little talk at the university had brought the demonstrators to graffiti up the town. And then he tried to act as a knight in shining armor and save her in distress. She didn't need any man doing that, especially a gringo.

Merc was about to find out how much this bothered Gabriela Cortez. This ridiculous agent in front of her, this joker, was going to become an instrument to demonstrate her wrath. Senor eagle would be useful.

Gaby lit up her best smile. "You know, if anything comes up around here, you could probably find it on the sandspit at Punta Gringa. That's two miles south. You should check out the trailers there. I think you might find the kind of community you are looking for. But don't tell anyone I mentioned this to you."

"I won't" Enrique was pleased. *This is how my father would have picked up on the clues.* He winked at Gaby but she couldn't have been colder. She ignored his outstretched hand, turned around and went back to her papers.

Enrique returned to the cab of the 4 Runner. Now, the ejido woman had mentioned the sandspit. Captain

Dolan demanded he check the place out. Focusing on that location would be a fertile place to start. He tuned the radio to the San Felipe pop music station. *This feels good. I'm picking up intel. I'm back in business as a field agent.*

22

Resurrection

Doc had been dead exactly a month on the morning he walked back into town.

He looked like hell—disheveled beard, ripped clothes, one shoe missing and about thirty pounds lighter. Unsteady along the unpaved road shoulder, he staggered around parked pickups and boat trailers and waved to pedestrians and drivers.

A panguero double-parked his truck. "Gracias a Dio," he said. "It's our dead Doc."

No question about it. It was Doc.

Yes, he was supposed to be dead. Murdered. Burned up. The police were sure they found his body weeks ago. Friends and enemies sang and wept at a memorial. His longtime partner Rose abandoned Punta Gringa and fled north of the border. Doc's associates descended on his home and divided up his CD and DVD collections, absconded with his pistols and rifles, reclaimed his favorite chaise lounges from his patio, and made off with his old dirt bike motorcycle, outboard skiff and his jet-ski. The ejido pilfered his furniture. Together, friend and foe cleaned the cupboard bare.

But now, here he stood, breathing like any human being, a bit rocky but very much alive and in good spirits, shading his eyes against the bright noon sun and chatting with passersby. His abductors, he was telling everyone, were two very smelly low life criminals. They had car-jacked his pickup and kept him prisoner in a fish camp somewhere south of Puertecitos. He said that when they burned the shack at the road junction, they had confused the police by leaving his wallet and dog tags beside the body of a smuggler from Belize who had died of snakebite while in Mexico. Doc's escape came two nights ago when he discovered that his kidnappers had disappeared.

Resurrection can be exciting. A return from the dead never happened before in Playa Refugio. The Miracle Doc soon was engulfed in a swarm of handshakes and abrazos, the Mexican back-clapping greeting. The pious wanted to touch him, then make the sign of the cross and say a prayer. Eventually, Doc felt lightheaded, so he bypassed the suspect food at the Loncheria and crossed the street to the El Parador where Ismael rushed out and almost knocked him over with a heart-felt abrazo. Ismael was in tears. He pulled the chair out for Doc.

"Thank God you're alive."

"You can say that again. I'm hungry."

"Get the Doc's favorite eggs," Ismael yelled to the kitchen. "Orange juice?"

"Thanks, Ismael. It is good to see you. Have you been well?"

"Of course. But I haven't been dead," grinned Ismael.

"Me neither." Doc grinned. "Okay. I'd love some food. But I seem to be short of pesos right now."

"No problem."

A kitchen helper came with a pitcher of fresh-squeezed juice.

"You know we thought you were gone forever," said Ismael.

"That's what I've heard."

"We had a beautiful memorial for you."

"Did people say nice things?"

"They did. Even the fish inspector."

"Old Rosales. That old bastard. He's fined me two hundred times."

"But you never paid. Anyway, there was great singing and pictures and plenty of desert lilies. Even Gaby said pleasant things about you."

"That's bizarre. I wish I was there."

Everyone surrounded Doc's table. Gaby hustled over from the ejido office across the street. She had tears in her eyes and gave Doc a big hug. "I'm so glad," she said with a huge smile. "But don't take this as a sign you are in my good graces."

Doc smiled back. "I enjoyed the hug but would never expect to be in your good graces, my sweet scorpion."

The crowd was growing larger. They wanted stories. They wanted details. They wanted to know if he had seen the white light at the end of the shrouded tunnel, and what heaven (or hell) had been like. In between bites, Doc kept embellishing the story. Yes, he had seen the white light. No, he hadn't had time to get to heaven or hell, but instead was kept in a six-by-six-foot shed in the fish camp.

Death had not dampened his appetite. He wolfed down a full order of scrambled eggs, bacon, salsa, beans and rice, and drank the pulpy fresh-squeezed orange juice and two cups of El Parador's heavenly coffee and steamed milk concoction café olé. For the crowd now surrounding his table, he rambled on until he finally tired. Ismael brought his truck around and gave the Miracle Doc a ride back to Punta Gringa.

Doc's resurrection was only two hours old when it went viral on the Internet. Facebook pages carried cell-phone pictures taken by everyday Refugians standing next to the reincarnated one. The regional radio and television stations sniffed out the news and slammed the story into the lead spot, shrieking about the miracle. Finally, most of the Southwestern tabloids and even respectable news-papers on both sides of the border splashed this across the front page. "Miraculous Return from the Dead" screamed one paper. "He's Alive" was the tabloid headline in another.

It was the end of June news doldrums, and so a herd of reporters and television news crews began making the two-hour drive south across the desert to suck up juicy details available only in Punta Gringa. At first, the atten-tion was amusing and Doc continued to fabricate details. But as more and more reporters slid to a stop in front of his house on the sandspit, he began to dodge them. He had learned his lesson about embellishing stories. Would he hold a press conference later? Nothing doing. Finally, to escape the badgering news jackals, he curled up in the back of Shay's old Oldsmobile, and with RJ riding shotgun, all three fled to Puertecitos, where they hid out for two days with friends who lived by the harbor.

Doc called Rose, who was now living in Yuma. She shrieked and howled. He wanted her to come to Punta Gringa but she refused. If he wanted her, she demanded, he would have to come to Arizona. That was final. Doc promised to make a trip north in a day or so, as soon as he was strong enough.

Doc's revival might have been sensational, but in Refugio, as happens in journalism anywhere, another news item rises up to take its place. And now there were rumors about an expansion of the battery recycling plant. If that happened, they would need another shift of workers and possibly more factory space on the Punta Gringa sandspit.

The proposed plant enlargement had been a strategic goal of a dissident ejido faction led by Alex Lopez. Gaby confirmed the plans and said she would reveal what she knew at a community gathering next week.

Merc was livid. Enlarging the plant would be the death knell for the sandspit community. That would be outrageous. When he was in town, he confided to Ismael. "She won't get away with it."

"What are you going to do?"

"Confront her. Give her a ration of shit."

"Go easy. This wasn't her idea."

"Horseshit. That woman would run over her mother to pimp this town."

Merc spied Gaby on the street outside the ejido

office, and started yelling about the evictions. Gaby walked over to his table at the El Parador. "Merc," she said, "calm yourself. I am not the one. You probably will have to deal with Alex Lopez and his friends. They've got risky development plans and they are throwing me out as ejido manager. After eight years. The executive session is in two days. I am not invited. You'll need to make friends with them."

"Is that for sure?"

"Pretty likely."

"I am so sorry to hear that."

"There is one piece of good news. Padre Nacho pulled through. He is coming out of the worst of it and the doctors say his heart is strong."

"So, La Gringa pulled it off."

"She did. She treated him with herbs, music and the power of love and it worked."

Gaby gave Merc a forlorn smile before she turned and walked away.

23

Too Many Questions

"Mercury Stiles. Merc?"

Merc had landed the Loncheria's prime table for his coffee—on the beach beneath a canvas canopy.

Now a stranger was standing next to him. Merc stared at the man's clothing. Gaudy running shoes. A freshly-pressed button-down dress shirt and plaid shorts. Unnatural here. It looked as if he had just been dropped into Baja from an LL Bean church service.

"Hi. I'm Nick. From L.A."

Merc slipped a spoon as a bookmark into the pages of his well-worn Wallender novel. The Swedish detective was struggling with a case.

"Hi."

"Mind if I sit down?"

"Do I know you?"

"Not really."

"Then don't sit down. Look, I don't mean to be rude, but I'm interested in this book."

"Uh. Sorry to bother you. The receptionist up the street said I should talk to you."

"The receptionist?"

"Yeah. Saucy little Mexican number named Gabriela."

Merc had never thought of Gaby as saucy. "She runs this village."

"Well, I was inquiring about fishing here. She said you were the one to ask."

Merc didn't know where this was going. "You'd be better off asking a local boat captain or any panguero. Try at the bait counter at the convenience store next door."

Merc looked back at the book. Nick remained standing at his table. "Heard you have a manta ray out there. Amazing."

"We had one. But he's left...and so should you."

Nick didn't move. "Pretty nice weather today."

No one in his right mind would describe blistering June heat as nice weather. "It's really too hot," said Merc. The intruder was getting irritating.

"Well, I like it. But, man, I hate the drive. On and on across the desert. Not a soul if you broke down. Not even a cactus. But this kind of heat is no problem. I dig it."

Dig it, thought Merc. *Haven't heard that for a thousand years.*

Nick tried another approach. "Hey Merc. I'm thirsty. Order a drink and I'll buy."

Merc's tact was fading. "Look, Nick, or whoever you are. I'll go up and order a coffee. I'll order one for you if you go find yourself a fucking table and leave me alone?"

"Sure. I'll take a Pacifico."

"At 10:30 in the morning? A Pacifico?"

"Sure. Here's a U.S tenner."

"Whatever." Merc walked over to the counter and ordered the drinks. Before he returned to the table, he spotted Señora Gabriela walking up the street. She smiled at him and stepped inside. Her rose perfume was particularly strong today.

"Merc. Heard the news about Padre Nacho?"

"How's he doing?"

"He is better. La Gringa nursed him around the clock. For two weeks without a break. He can sit up in bed and walk a little."

Gaby nodded over toward Nick. "I see you've met that pushy gringo. He was in my office, asking questions. And he knew your name. Asked how to get in touch with you."

"Did you tell him I knew a lot about fishing?"

"No. He said he couldn't speak Spanish. So I told him to ask any ex-pat he saw."

She switched to a grim expression. "Merc. Stay in touch. Something else is happening. We need to talk later." And with this ominous warning, Gaby walked back out into the street. Merc returned to his to his table.

"I see you were yakking with what's her name," Nick said.

Merc handed him the change. "Gabriela. Now leave, please. I'm going back to my book."

"I'm off to Puertecitos. Where in Puertecitos can I get the local fishing tips?"

Merc paused. "CowPatty's. It's on your right as you pull into town. The locals there can recommend competent boat captains. And if you catch a few Locos, they can cook up anything you catch."

"That's bitchin. I'd love to get a Loco. I hear they put up quite a fight. So, what do you do here? Where are you from?"

"Well, Nick. I really don't do anything here."

Nick paused. "Yes you do. You are an environmentalist. I checked out your blog before I came down."

The waiter brought a café ole and a beer. But two overloaded stake trucks rumbled into the town. Merc jumped up, ran out to the street, took out his miniature video camera and started shooting. He panned the camera as the vehicles sped by, stirring up dust. They were headed for the outlet road to Punta Gringa.

The video got better. The trailing truck hit the gaping pothole near the Loncheria and bounced wildly, sending two used batteries crashing to the street. Unaware he had lost part of his load, the driver continued on out of town.

Merc was ecstatic. He took closeups of the fallen batteries. "Did you see that? That kind of stuff—batteries falling off the trucks—it happens all the time. That'll make the blog today."

Nick was surprised. "What the hell. He didn't even stop to pick it up."

"That's right. I've found old broken batteries all the way to the plant. They used to bring a truckload a day. Now, it's two and sometimes three trucks every morning."

Nick was still standing by the table. He took a swig of the beer. "Well, I'm surprised how much trash is everywhere in Mexico. It's all over the place." He paused. "By the way, you could help me out. I'm looking for an old friend from L.A."

Merc ignored him. "The Mexicans say there isn't any danger. I guess lead poisoning isn't supposed to affect old fart foreigners."

"Yeah. But maybe you could help me. I am really looking for my old friend. His name is James or Jim. Very religious guy?"

"Look, Nick, no offense, but you need to leave."

"I'd be happy to pay you for this information."

"Goodbye, Nick."

Nick drained his beer. "Well, I should go. Keep up the blog. I'll keep reading it. Maybe I'll catch you on the way back."

Not if I can help it, thought Merc. *Clearly there were too many questions.*

After lunch, Merc took the dirt road towards Punta Gringa. A thin column of black smoke was rising from a small outbuilding behind the battery recycling plant. The offshore wind was blowing it into the hills. Merc whipped out the camcorder and shot from the overlook at the head of the grade. When he had thirty seconds of the wispy smoke, he jumped back in the pickup and headed for the factory. At the main gate, he checked in with the guard and then slowly crawled in low gear along the sandy path that circled the plant. He stopped behind the small outbuilding and began shooting more video.

Francisco Arcangel came out and walked up to him.

"At it again, Merc?"

"Yeah, I thought I'd finish the fire stuff."

"Well, you'll find nothing there. It was just cleaning supplies. But you can take all you want. Even inside. I hope you are honest in your blog and mention it was soap and stuff."

Later, Merc downloaded the video into a computer at the Internet hot spot in the Acosta's grocery store. He edited out a minute or so before posting to YouTube the portion showing the trucks, the batteries crashing to the street and the first smoke. He added text that the plant officials explained the fire was in a supply cabinet. Finally, he linked it to his blog. This stuff was exciting. It should stir things up.

Relaxing under his palapa was next on the agenda. The heat was terrible. Also, there was a very immediate need to warn RJ about this dirtbag named Nick. The man might be on RJ's trail. That would explain the questions. Nick wasn't a fisherman, that's for sure. There wasn't a fish in Baja called a Loco.

24

Enrique's Misstep

Merc's video showing the fire was powerful. The blog stirred mangers in the PROFEPA office in Mexico City to send an agent to check on it. When Merc arrived back to Punta Gringa after coffee the next day, he found Veronica standing in his driveway, using her long metal wand to take air and ground samples.

"Ah, bienvenidos, Veronica. How'd you find my place?"

She smiled. "Don't be so rude. Any competent Mexican woman could do it. It would have been easier if you had invited me." She set down her backpack. "Now, let's be more pleasant. I'll start." She softened her voice. "Why, hello, Merc. I'm still pissed. They sent me to investigate the pollution that might have come from the silly little truck incident you posted on YouTube. I flew all the way to this fleabag sandspit because some boss in Mexico City saw your blog. So, I just thought I'd stop and tell you why this trip here makes me mad."

Merc didn't relax. "Hello. Sorry you had to come a

long way but it's about time you guys were concerned."

"Look, you've got to understand we have around 20 battery plants to check and this one is the cleanest," she said. "So, don't be so critical."

"Ok. You're right. The criticism stops now."

Veronica smiled and began loading the backpack into her rental car.

"Well, I'm done," she said.

"With everything today?"

"Si. Off to the airport in Mexicali. I've got five hours before my plane leaves."

"That's a two-hour drive. You look pretty dusty. Would you like to wash up a bit? You can use my sink."

"You have one?"

"Very funny."

"Yes, I'd like that," she said.

Merc could see Veronica was in the game. She was smart and playful. "After you clean up, do you have time for a coffee or a beer?"

"Love a cold soda now."

"Coca lite?"

"Perfecto. Gracias."

Merc returned from the kitchen with two glasses. "Sorry, no ice, but there is no way to keep it out here. The soda, though, is cool." He handed her a glass.

Veronica took a sip. "It's fine. As long as it is wet, that's great."

She paused and turned to watch four pelicans resting on the beach ten feet from Merc's patio. The afternoon light spread a golden glow across the coastline. "It's very beautiful here," she said, gazing at the water. "I can see why you love this patio."

"That's why I built this house."

"You built this casita."

"Well, most of it. Friends helped. Yeah. Before that, I lived in that disgusting trailer over there," he said, pointing to the nearby Streamlite sitting up on blocks.

"Where did you get the wood? It's expensive here."

"Bought a little in San Felipe but I brought most from the U.S."

"That must have cost you. Customs duty and all."

"Promise you won't arrest me." Merc lowered his voice to a conspiratorial tone. "I smuggled a lot of it in. I used an old flatbed truck. Made the wood into a box and put junky stuff like chairs in the box. The border people thought that the box was part of the truck and the junk was what I was bringing in."

"So then, you took the box apart and built the house."

"That's right."

"Hey, you recycled. That's very Mexican. That's what a Mexican would have done."

"Well, this spot is special. I was hoping to stay here for a long time. Then came the battery plant. Pepe the manta ray. And then these crazy drones and now this plane crash."

"Well, we always worry about factories like yours across the road. It's just that this one, I don't know, is so clean."

"Meaning?"

"Meaning we don't know. The plant is a gold medal example of what a plant should be."

No one spoke for a full minute. Both stared out to

the water. Finally, Veronica said she had better wash up. She went to her car and returned with a spare shirt.

Merc showed her the outdoor basin and the enclosure behind the house. It had no roof but was shielded by a circular five-foot high stone wall built with desert rocks. "I'm afraid it's open air but because it almost never rains here, it'll do."

The washstand was a homebuilt job. White plastic pipe brought in cold water from the rooftop tank and joined a pipe carrying hot water from a wood burner. Merc lit the firewood, showed her how to adjust the cold and the hot, and added a caution to use as little as possible.

The rock enclosure also served as a clothesline. Two pairs of jeans and three of his undershorts flapped in the breeze on a rope stretched across the sink. Veronica was amused. She pointed to his well-worn fish-print boxers, ancient ones with holes in them. "I love your dryer. This is very rustic but by the condition of things, you need to get to the store." And she laughed.

Merc quickly pulled his undershorts off the line. "Rustic is only in the mind of the city-dweller. These get the job done." He handed her a new bar of soap and a clean towel. "When you are finished, meet you by the beach. I'll get chips and salsa ready."

Veronica waited until Merc was back on the patio. She removed her polo shirt and her bra, hung them on a nail, and began to wash, unaware she was not alone.

—ᚠ—

Enrique had been motivated to bust his case wide open. He was working two new leads. Captain Dolan wanted him to check out the suspicious sandspitter named Doc and the ejido boss Gabriela Cortez had pointed him this way. Punta Gringa, then, was a good place to start. He hid the 4-Runner by the road and climbed down a cliff to set up a surveillance position on the bluff above the sandspit homes. From here he could surreptitiously watch all the comings and goings in the community.

Castillo believed agents needed to be comfortable. He came well stocked with supplies. After inflating his portable stadium seat cushion, he set out his binoculars, a few energy bars, three bottles of water and a battery powered video game player. Now he was ready to spend untold hours in his catbird seat, checking out the action below.

For a while, it was quiet. About two-thirty, a Mexican woman arrived wearing tight jeans, a hardhat and an emergency reflective vest. She parked next to one house, got out with a backpack, and started to collect samples. Castillo focused the binoculars. She was hot.

Next, an old pickup rattled in, driven by a slim man with a goatee. It pulled up to the same house. The pair had a long discussion before they went inside. The man took the woman around to the shower and washstand area that was behind the house. Enrique could easily see over the wall. The man took a few clothes off the line, went into the house and returned to the patio.

In no time, agent Castillo was getting more than he bargained for. Once the man left, the woman took off her top and her bra, apparently was ready to wash up.

It had been several months since Sylvia left and now Enrique was stalled in a non-voluntary celibate life, bereft of tenderness or touching. Here, in dusty Punta Gringa, deep in Mexico, in the afternoon under a wilting sun, he was getting a show, a bonus for long hours of gritty everyday surveillance of drug gangs. True, she was a bit older, but she was in buff shape.

The woman began to wash methodically, splashing water on her brown body, and languorously rubbing soap in her armpits and across the back of her neck. She seemed to be enjoying the sunshine on her skin. Her broad shoulders and small but attractive breasts reminded him of Sylvia.

Enrique was fascinated. She began to gently caress her chest with the soap. *This, he thought, is better than some of those Internet sites.*

A warm feeling was rising. How long had it been? His unwanted solitary life had deprived him of those blissful moments he shared with Sylvia. He absentmindedly started to stroke the outside of his jeans. To no one in particular he said. "Oh yeah, wash those again and again. Oh yeah. Nice body." Castillo loosened his belt. He spit on his hand and was moving it toward his waist. He felt the first rapturous waves...then...whack.

And the lights went out.

25

Red Ants

Rapturous throbbing was the last agent Castillo remembered before regaining consciousness in an ancient barn. He was sitting on straw, his head ached and his wrists were sore where ropes now bound him to an animal's stall door. A mangy German shepherd dog with a scabby skin rash, foul breath and crusty yellow teeth was standing at the side, slobbering and staring at him. The dog kept trying to lick his false mustache. When Enrique yelled, the dog growled. Enrique kept motionless.

Hijole, this place smells like a stable. Like cowshit, he thought, *like goats. Where the fuck am I?* He banged against the stall wall, struggling with his restraints.

A woman with lupine grey eyes and a corona of wild brown hair came in. She trailed an aroma like oranges on a warm day.

"So you are awake?" She was speaking English with no accent.

"Yes. Where am I?"

"At a goat farm."

"Por favor. Do you have water?"

"I do."

"Por favor, may I have a little?"

"Eventually."

"Where is this farm?"

"In the canyons near Playa Refugio."

"Why do you have me tied up?"

"You are lucky you are not dead. When I found you, you were spying on people, watching women take their shirts off. You had opened your pants and were playing with your corncob. I had to hit you with my goat stick. You are a pervert. How can you be this great man's son?"

"Great man's son?"

"You wallet says you are Enrique Castillo. I knew El Toro Castillo and I knew he had a son named Enrique. You look like him. I am a curandera. I treated many of El Toro's scorpion stings, insect bites, and infected cuts from cactus spines. He was a tough, honest man who battled the scourge of cocaine. He worked with people. He never sent the poor to jail—just the rich. But you. The product of his loins. Your head is only clouded with desire. You, you are a disgrace."

Not again, thought Enrique. *Someone else who knew dad.* And then he spotted it. There it was, on the stable wall, framed next to pictures of Jesus Christ and Buddha, there was the famous inside book jacket picture of El Toro Castillo, autographed to "Athena."

This must be the legendary Gringa of Punta Gringa. The events that morning started to come back to him. Everything that happened. So, a sorceress captured him. Could she really have done it all by herself?

His head throbbed. His pants were sticky.

"Do you have any aspirin?"

"No."

"I have a terrible headache."

"I am starting a fire in this old fuel drum. The smoke will cure your head."

The stench increased. "What are you burning? It smells like dead people."

"It's waste from the goats' stables. Mixed with hay. This kind of smoke will treat your urges." La Gringa used a newspaper to fan the smoke in his direction.

"It stinks. Will you untie me? I can pay you." He coughed as if he was choking.

"No."

Castillo coughed again. "What is going to happen? The smoke smells awful. It is poisonous."

"It is necessary because I have to medicate your evil side," she said as she began to unlace and remove his boots.

"What are you doing with my feet?"

"I am going to apply an old cure. I learned this from my *maestra*—my teacher—that the bite of red ants would lessen your perverted cravings."

"What the hell are you doing?" pleaded Enrique.

The curandera left the barn and returned with a jar. "I have captured very smart red ants. I will shake them up to make them angry. Then I will pour a few onto your bare skin. The bites will release a potion to cool down your urges."

"Don't you…" But the curandera with the lupine eyes scattered the irate ants onto his feet. Six or seven began crawling in between the toes, biting his skin.

It hurt like hell. "Yeawwwww," he yelled. "What the fuck are you doing? Yeawwww. I will get the police after you."

"They'll be here soon. I have called the rurales—the local police. You will have to wait, pervert." And La Gringa watched him howl and scream for a few minutes.

After that, the healer who once had cured the lesions of the most celebrated, toughest border agent of Northern Baja, a man she had admired, cleaned the ants off his feet, closed the lid on the jar and walked out the door. Enrique was left to stew in his anxiety. What if the captain heard about this little episode? The captain would be furious and upset. His co-workers would have a field day.

Enrique relaxed a bit. He could hear goats braying outside, as if they, too, were disappointed in him.

26

A Warning

"I see you have a very appreciative letter from the government," said Luis, the dourer of the two Acosta brothers who ran the Playa Refugio grocery and mail drop.

Merc smiled. "Luis, someday I'd love to get some mail that wasn't opened."

"We never open anything."

"That's bullshit, Luis. I know you've already read it. Hand over the envelope from the government investigators." The letter inside was in English and referred to the plane crash two weeks ago.

"We want to thank you for providing us with the visual materials and an eyewitness account in relation to the recent crash of an airplane near Playa Refugio. We have downloaded the video and are returning your memory chip."

"The Cessna 404 had suffered an engine failure on takeoff due to ingestion of wind blown debris. The pilots turned sharply to avoid the village of Playa Refugio and crashed into the sea. Both pilots survived."

"There were many witnesses to the tragic plunge of the Cessna. All their stories and accounts will be used to recreate the last moments for the plane, including your accounts of the Bat-Mex divers retrieving items from the wreckage."

"We appreciate your assistance."

That was it. Merc was frustrated. Nowhere did they mention what was in the 20 bags of contraband the Bat Mex divers brought from the wreckage.

So much bullshit, he thought. Everyone who had flocked to the crash site could guess that Bat-Mex workers were absconding with a suspicious cargo.

Merc headed to the lunch patio at El Parador. He sat alone outside, re-reading the note. Nearby, Bat-Mex crews were busy scrubbing the week-old anti-recycling graffiti off the walls. When he looked up, Francisco Arcangel was sitting opposite him.

"Relaxing, Merc?"

"Trying to. When I'm not bothered."

"Well, I just wanted to let you know that I'm mad."

"And...I should worry?"

"Merc, you've finally gotten your wish. You got to me by bringing the protestors down here to paint ugly graffiti all over the town and I had to pay to get it cleaned off. But above that, you have spurred the government into investigating my battery plant. I can't tell you how that pisses me off."

"You know I didn't have anything to do with the graffiti business and you know it was the crash of your company plane that brought the investigators. So get off my back."

"No. I blame you. And now the federales are beating a different drum. They have agents contacting my workers, trying to get them to make incriminating statements about what goes on at the plant."

"Francisco, what can I do about that?"

"Merc, after the stupid manta ray jumped around as if he was high, everyone suspected some drugs got into the water from my plane."

"Francisco. That's where the drugs came from. It's hard to imagine Pepe bought his drugs from a street dealer."

"Very funny. The truth is the federales found big quantities of bagged methamphetamines—speed—in the plane. Unknown to me, the pilots were smuggling substantial quantities of this material. It apparently flooded into the seawater."

"Tell that to Pepe, our speed freak manta. I'm sure he is still going to meetings, trying to get sober. Francisco, I just got a note from the crash investigators. It didn't say anything about drugs."

"Of course they wouldn't put that in the official reports. The pilots were heroes because they saved the village. Big heroes. Mexico needs good stories. Listen, the investigators will talk to you again. I hope you will be honest."

"Francisco, I don't talk to investigators. I shouldn't have given them my video of the divers retrieving bags from the crashed plane. I was worried about lead pollution from your batteries. About any other cargo, I don't even want to speculate. We gringos in Mexico should be smart enough to keep our noses out of that kind of business. If they ask me about pollution, you know I will show them my readings and tell them what I think. If they ask me about anything else, I know nothing. Nothing. I guarantee that."

"Good, just so we understand each other. It could be dangerous." Francisco stood and left with his bodyguards.

That was strange, thought Merc. A very direct threat. Francisco actually adding the bit about the drugs. That made it all the more suspicious. But Merc was not getting involved. Period. End of story.

Later, while he finished his breakfast on the patio, he saw soldiers stop a truck headed to the battery plant. They searched the cargo and then waved the truck on. That was the first time he could remember anyone being worried about what was in those trucks.

Merc sensed that events were starting to spin out of control. He might have to pack up his things. Whatever happened, it looked like he would have to prepare for the worst.

27

Castillo's Legend

Twenty-four hours after he was whacked on the head, two burly San Felipe police officers arrived and released Agent Castillo from his barnlike prison. La Gringa had summoned them. He stunk from pissing in his pants and his feet were swollen with insect bites. They laughed when he wanted to press charges.

"She poured ants on my feet. It was cruel."

"You say ants. I don't see any ants."

"I want her arrested. Look at the bites," and he pointed to his feet.

The police ignored him. "Could be mosquitoes. So you are the son of the famous El Toro?"

"Yes, I am."

"Well, you must be the little calf, El Becerro. Your father would never have done what you did. You should learn that this is a frontier place and not everything people do can be hidden behind private walls. Sometimes we relieve ourselves on a cactus. Sometimes we wash ourselves in the open. It is polite to respect another's virtue in these private moments. Look the other way. Don't take pleasure in it. Don't try to whack off. Don't do this again or we might let the locals think up their own brand of justice."

"But what about the ants. The torture. Burning goat shit in the room."

"These are just treatments for perverts. We hope they work."

"So you won't arrest her?"

"Are you kidding? She cares for many of our problems."

"Am I free to go?"

"Claro—sure. It might be a mortal sin but there's no criminal law against playing with yourself." The two officers grinned at each other and exchanged high fives.

"So, where am I? Where is this goat farm?"

"You should know La Gringa's place. Everyone does. It is about a mile back to the highway."

"Hey. Will you take me back to my truck? It's near Punta Gringa."

"We just cleaned the back seat of the car. Your kind of filth will make it dirty. You can walk to your truck. It will give you time to think about what you did." Both officers laughed again, returned to their squad car and drove off.

Castillo hiked from the remote goat farm to the road, got his bearings, and continued another mile or so back to where his truck had been hidden. It was long gone. *Oh crap,* he thought, *that belongs to Border Protection. What do I do now?*

He continued around the rocks and down to the spot where he had been captured. His arena seat cushion, satellite phone with a dead battery, backpack with his i.d. and the Glock were still there.

Now he had to hike the two miles to Playa Refugio in the sweltering heat. Food was on his mind but he had other problems. His satellite phone was dead. His department issued undercover vehicle had been ripped off. A slobbering dog had licked off his fake mustache. His feet had painful lesions. And worst of all—his personal dignity was in tatters.

On the plus side, Enrique still had enough pesos, a few energy bars and his Glock, which had been hidden in his backpack.

The soldiers at the roadside checkpoint harassed him, wondering what crazy fool would be out walking in the blistering sun on a road where everyone else drives. They checked his identification and confirmed that he was an agent with Customs and Border Protection. That information got his pack through the roadblock without an inspection. If they had found his pistol, they might not have been so forgiving.

Once in town, he sensed that everyone was smirking. The villagers seemed to know what had happened. The San Felipe police had obviously stopped in Refugio and spilled the beans. His run in with the La Gringa, and her knockout blow with her shepherd's crook while he was whacking off—well, that was the talk of the town.

Castillo felt defiled. Mortified. Even worse, he had blown his undercover identity. This was a critical setback for an agent. Once everyone knew he worked for the anti-narco squads, no one would ever speak to him again.

He had to talk to Dolan. The local Internet café inside Acosta's grocery store was the only public phone. Castillo knew somebody might be listening to his conversation.

Still, he had to get in touch. He paid 200 pesos to use Acosta's satellite landline.

"Dolan please."

"Dolan."

"It's Castillo. I must warn you. I'm on a public phone."

"What about your company mobile?"

"Battery is dead."

The captain laughed. "Well, you'd better get it charged up. We've heard from the local police. It seems you've been quite busy in the field. Sort of caught with your pants down. And not by the bad guys."

"I've been busy. I'm onto some critically vital information. But first, tell me, what happened with the Nevada boys and the grim reapers."

"Castillo, we can't discuss that on this phone." That captain paused. "But here is something that needs tracking down. Our company is looking for anyone there who can repair fiberglass. We want them to patch up one of our fishing boats."

"Fixing fiberglass? On our boat? What are you talking about?"

"Think about it, Castillo."

Enrique paused. The light began to shine. "Oh yeah, I understand now, a fiberglass…oh yeah. I understand. Is there anything else you can tell me?"

"Not much on a public phone. The San Felipe police forwarded to us the official report about your indiscretions."

"I was doing surveillance of a village."

"That's not what the police down there wrote to us. Do you still have the truck?"

Castillo swallowed. "Yes, it seems to be okay."

"That's odd. Because this morning we caught two Playa Refugio tweaks with an identical truck trying to cross the border at Calexico with ten kilos of weed."

"Just like my truck? There are a lot of 4 Runners that look like it down here. Are you sure?"

"Not just like your truck. It was your truck. In fact, it still had your radios in it and the same vehicle identification number as the truck we gave you. The driver was wearing your department-issued baseball cap."

"Okay. My truck was stolen too."

"We guessed that." The Captain paused. "Castillo, you're becoming an a-list number one screw-up. And I'm getting heat from above on this too."

"What do you think I should do now?"

"I can't say. Not on this phone. Your father, God rest his soul, your father, El Toro, never lost a vehicle. You can be thankful the truck was only an impound."

"Informally, what's my next step? I'm very close to cracking this case."

"You need to return to San Felipe."

"Why?"

"Actually, a couple of our agents have already been in Refugio. We've checked some leads there. So I think it's time that you come back to Yuma. There will be a disciplinary hearing. Your disgraceful capture by a mystic healer has been the talk of the office. My boss is raging mad about it. And, I might add, you are making us the laughingstock of the entire Southwest District."

"Captain, I'm getting close to solving this case."

"Castillo, get real. You are not getting close to solving this case. You are doing a pretty good job of fucking it up. With you on the ground, we end up with extra work. You need to come back. Can you get to San Felipe?"

"Captain, are you going to fire me?"

"I don't know what the outcome from the hearing will be."

"Captain, I don't want to come back without solving this."

"Castillo, you have to come back. That's an order."

"But Captain, I love this job."

"Yes, I know that. But your little incident was a major screw-up in the field. All you are doing now is making a mess. Antagonizing people. We can't afford that."

"Okay, I'll come back but I have to check out that ex air force guy first."

"I'm ordering you to come back now."

"It'll take me a couple of days to get to San Felipe.

"Leave right now."

"I have to find a ride. It'll take two days."

"No."

"Okay, I'll go see if I can find a ride. But it might take time."

"Do your best."

"Oops. Out of time. Gotta go." And Enrique hung up

Castillo was crushed. Now he deserved the nickname of El Becerro, the young calf. This could also be the end of his cushy drone flying days and the end of his drug-hunting adventures. It would be very embarrassing.

But before any return to San Felipe, he had a mis-guided urge to probe the Punta Gringa community again. Among the shacks there, he remembered a sign for fiber-glass repair for boats. If fiberglass was a clue, maybe someone who worked with that material could lead him to the Cubans and the cartel drone attackers. Then he could keep his job.

Yes, he needed to go back to Punta Gringa.

28

The Record Books

Today's drone mission appeared very ordinary on the surface. The air force pilots were to fly the Border Protection Predators on routine anti-drug patrols two miles off the Sea of Cortez coast. Above them, the more powerful Reaper drones would be lurking as bodyguards. One Reaper carried cameras to record any intercept and the other was armed with two experimental Skyfire missiles, ready to smoke the intruder. These weapons had been tested but had not been used in actual combat. The atmosphere in the trailers was tense—you could say there was an aura of destiny. If the cartel was greedy and careless, today's crew might be part of a milestone in the era of remotely piloted aircraft combat.

"Charley 2 is two miles south of Puertecitos. No boats in sight. I'm going to bring him back toward the coastline."

The day commander stood behind the pilot. "You can do that. This is the dangerous location for intercepts."

Charley 2 was only westbound for a minute when the Reaper video bodyguard spotted a tiny aircraft slip in above the Predator.

"We have a bogey. It's in position on top of the Predator."

"If we have video, and our Predator is protected from the missile lock-on, then let's go with Bird Strike," said the day commander. The Reaper weapons officer armed its Skyfires, finalized the target protocols and begin tracking the intruder.

As the foreign drone moved slowly downward to settle in a position just above the Predator, the bodyguard Reaper set it up in its digital crosshairs.

"Colonel, I need permission to fire," asked the pilot.

"That's affirmative," was the response. "You may execute."

The Reaper's armament co-pilot confirmed the shot. By now, the entire team at Creech gathered around the monitors, watching in silence. The Reaper launched a single Skyfire. It streaked toward the Courtesan and scored a bulls-eye hit on the delta-winged invader, demolishing it with a crisp explosion. Charley 2 appeared to be untouched.

Cheers echoed through the trailers at the air base. Two Reaper controllers jumped up, ran toward each other and chest bumped in celebration. They were part of aviation history—the first air-to-air drone warfare in the region.

Following the attack, the pilots returned all the drones back to Nevada. Colonel Perkins called for a post mortem in a briefing room stocked with cases of beer and snacks from the base café.

The commanders were justly proud of their drone's air-to-air strike against the enemy drone. The Skyfire had been accurate, picking off the attacker without leaving a scratch on the Predator less than five feet below it. By almost every standard, the destruction of the cartel's annoying anti-drone was a resounding success. The minor downside was the Skyfire's explosive power—it pulverized the attacking craft. From the replay, no one expected to find a single piece of wreckage larger than a corn flake.

Only one pilot, Customs and Border Protection liaison Harley Hooper, had any reservations. He studied the video over and over. Should he say anything? Should he spoil the party? The running time displays on the bottom of the monitors, showing the bodyguard Reaper firing the missile and the ensuing explosion above the Predator, were hard evidence. To Hooper, and he knew he could be wrong, it appeared the cartel's unusual looking delta wing drone exploded a half second before the Skyfire reached it. Impossible.

I must be seeing things, he thought. *Maybe there is an explanation.*

Hooper brought this up. When he pointed out the anomaly, no one paid attention. The general consensus— some sort of video time delay. A transmission artifact. After all, how could that happen unless the drone that attacked the Predator was rigged to explode?

—◊◊—

Back in his cave, H sat in a rumpled jumpsuit and relaxed in his lounge chair. He was not overly concerned about the Courtesan the Air Force thought they shot down. The attack confirmed his suspicions that they might experiment with an air-to-air missile. That's why he had sent up a very special, expendable Courtesan.

Maybe no one would realize he had recorded and transmitted the Skyfire's target lock-on protocols before blowing up the old model Courtesan. In the next days, he would write new code for his upcoming triumph—the double drone attack that would net him a Predator.

Right now, he was happy for the air force pilots. Glad they had a joyful moment when shooting at an old, worthless Courtesan. He had been in those trailers, sat through those post-mortems. They needed this shootdown to salve their egos. Enrique and his buddies were probably knuckle-bumping right now. Go ahead. Celebrate. Maybe now the Predator team and this Castillo guy would chill a bit and let their guard down.

29

Roadblocks

"You'll have to step out of the truck. Stand by the curb. Keep your hands up."

Merc wasn't used to a fifteen-year-old soldier poking him with an automatic weapon while his recruit buddies ransacked the pickup. Maybe at the permanent military checkpoint north of San Felipe but not under the wing of the life-size manta ray statue at the turnoff to Playa Refugio. Not in front of Pepe's ghost.

In the village, changes were obvious. The weather-beaten plywood had been pulled off the front of the abandoned convenience store on the main street. That mini-mart closed years ago after the owner surprised his wife in the storeroom playing with an employee's sweet potato. Now, the Mexican flag flew above the door and soldiers and grim faced men in suits waited outside. Three or four dusty official-looking government pickups were parked in front. Obviously, the federales had swarmed the town and were kicking off something big.

Merc sat at a veranda table at the El Parador patio to get a coffee and the morning wisdom from Ismael. He planned to quietly read his six-month-old New Yorker magazine. Four youngish muscular men with crew cuts sat nearby. One was watching Merc. *Crap. It's another gang of agents.* Merc guessed they were gringos—their accented Spanish giving them away. At this time of the morning, with so few locals on the streets, a naïve visitor might conclude that drug agents outnumbered the regular residents of Refugio.

Ismael delivered an espresso and whispered in a conspiratorial tone about the prosecutors from Mexico City that were in the village. "They are questioning everyone who works at the battery plant. No one," said Ismael, "has revealed anything yet."

Merc looked up, surprised to see that Gaby had slipped into the chair across the table from him. She was angry. "Merc. Hope you've noticed. We've got checkpoints everywhere. Our town is crawling with federal agents. Tourists and fishermen have stopped coming here. I say it's partly your fault. You've got to ease up in your blog about the battery plant."

Merc glanced briefly at her, and looked down at his magazine.

"Merc. Look at me. Don't ignore what I am saying." She looked peeved.

This time Merc locked onto her gaze. "Señora, get real. Don't blame me. You know this focus is not just on a battery plant but is something much bigger, something from the capital. You are smart enough to know that. In fact, I suspect you knew this crackdown was coming."

"Merc, I want you to know that Bat-Mex might close

the plant temporarily. Everyone will be out of work."

Merc raised his voice. "It was the Bat-Mex plane crash that made the government check out the plant. Not me. This is not about pollution. That's an old story. This is about Mexican criminals that I don't want anything to do with it. So, for all of us who desire to live a long life, this conversation is over."

"Merc, if they close the plant, my Refugians will blame you. That's what I have heard. It's not right, but they will. There is a lot of bad blood now. The situation could catch fire. I don't want you to get hurt."

Merc didn't know where to go with this. But he wasn't going to feign remorse. "You know, I think something else is going on here. I think that your battery plant, and its reliable salaries, has caused a great unrest in your remote fishing village. You thought that the new money would help Playa Refugio but maybe it changed the town. The younger workers want to leave dull, quaint Playa Refugio and move to better neighborhoods in San Felipe. Alex and his brothers, who will head the ejido, have even opened a chic restaurant on the beachfront malecon in San Felipe, not in Playa Refugio.

Gaby continued to stare blankly. "Yes, some of that may be true, Merc, and that is sad. Here's more. Tonight's the night for the takeover. By tomorrow, I will no longer be in charge. Alex and his associates want major development and if that happens, many Mexicans and gringos may have to move. There will be a carload of broken promises. That, I fear, is what in store for the sandspit."

"You mean the ejido needs the land for a bigger factory."

"Yes, or perhaps a condo development. Then they

can sell lots to rich Mexicans or gringos."

"Well, we ratas will have to deal with it," said Merc.

"Speaking of the ratas out there, have you seen RJ?"

"Sure. Almost every day."

"Well, remember that pushy investigator who was here asking about fishing? He's back. The gringo named Nick? The one who knew your name? Now he is asking about former ministers. I told him I didn't know of any. If you know any, you might warn him to hide out a bit and stop telling everyone that Jesus loves us."

"I certainly would pass that along if I knew of any."

"Oh, and by the way. Speaking of ministers, I saw Padre Nacho the other day. He's back in his pickup banging around the countryside tending to his flock. He limps badly but still has his foot. And he said to say hello to you and to thank you for your prayers."

"My prayers?" Merc looked incredulous.

Gaby broke into a wide smile. "Yes, I laughed too." She put out her hand, gently patted and deliberately stroked the back of Merc's, gave him a sly smile, rose from the chair and walked away.

Merc was jolted. He stared at his hand. Other than the moment he wrenched her free from the crazed mob during the battery protest, he had never had friendly physical contact with Gaby. Not even so much as a handshake. Her touch was an electric shock.

This latest news was mixed. The update on Padre Nacho was terrific. However, it was troubling that Alex was replacing Gaby in the ejido. She had been tough but honest. This ejido takeover would no doubt be the end of the sandspit's community. The beach would become vacation homes for the rich. To Merc, this was the equivalent of selling a soul to the devil.

The rest of his coffee time did not go smoothly. The general mood in town was surly. Drivers who used to wave hello ignored him or gave him the finger. Pedestrians didn't stop to chat. When he went into Acosta's store to buy a week's groceries, the clerk waited on the person behind him first. Everyone looked through Merc.

Returning to his pickup, he was overwhelmed by the aroma of citrus. Standing beside the driver's door was the curandera La Gringa. He hadn't seen her up close for years, not since his first day in Mexico. Her kindly face glowed behind her penetrating gray-green eyes.

"Mercury Stiles," she said in perfect English, "I had a vision and you are in danger. Something will happen in the Sal Si Puedes and you must be ready."

"La Gringa. You saved Padre Nacho. What a wonderful thing you did."

"Yes, he is walking again."

"I heard your name is Athena. She was the goddess of heroic endeavors."

"Yes, it is Athena." La Gringa paused. "But don't ignore the warning in this vision. The signs are not good." And she turned and walked away.

Merc drove back to the sandpit. For the moment, he enjoyed the lingering citrus aroma. Should he take the drug-induced visions of a sorceress and a medium? Still, he knew she must be on the right track. He had been very aware of the animosity in the town. How long before this might turn into violence?

Parking behind the old Streamlite trailer, he could

see that his back door was ajar and there was the mess inside. Someone had been through his desk and the boxes of his clothes stacked against the wall. His things had been thrown about. The intruder chalked slogans on the walls. "Sandspit for the Mexicans." The false wall behind the sink, though, hadn't been touched.

Merc would clean it up later. Before he could settle in, he had to make one more trip to Refugio tonight. It was the first Sunday night of the month and his regular dividend check was in his California account and available at a San Felipe ATM. It was time for the standing appointment he had with a special evening guest. He was looking forward to a very exhausting sensual night.

Right now, all he wanted was to open a Pacifico and relax for a few hours out on the patio. The sunset was behind him, and a pinkish haze had fallen on the Sea of Cortez. The hills glowed deep brownish-purple, a color unique to the moments before dusk. Flights of pelicans skimmed the water. This peace is how he wanted to remember it. From now on, it was going to be a rough ride.

30

The Door Closes

Merc was groggy and barely awake, standing out behind his house in the chill morning relieving himself on a mesquite bush. A car pulled up followed by an insistent banging at the front door. This couldn't be anyone from the sandspit—they wouldn't knock, they'd just barge in.

He wandered drowsily in through the back door, pulled on his pants, buttoned his shirt and shrugged his shoulders at his guest lounging about in bed. Her hair was in a wild state after a night of lovemaking She grinned and coyly maneuvered the covers up over her face. Before he reached the front door, there was more knocking. He opened it a tiny crack.

"Surprise." A buoyant Veronica was standing on his porch, dressed in white shorts and a form-fitting yellow top. Her hair was shaken loose and blew languidly in the breeze. She grinned. "I've got a hat this time."

Merc would freely admit she had done a thorough

job of ditching the rugged scientist look for a tasty makeover. "Yeah. Surprise."

"Well, aren't you happy to see me?"

"Yes, I am. Wow, you know, what a surprise." Merc peered secretively through the crack.

"I ran some final tests at the battery plant and thought I'd stop by for a coffee. I've got some very interesting news to tell you." There was a pause. "Are you going to ask me in?"

"It's…uhm…not exactly a perfect time."

"Make it a good time. Wait until you hear this. This news should change your life. You…you will like it."

"Okay." Merc smiled weakly, stepped aside and the now stylish Veronica strode into the simple room. Clothes were everywhere. The vandal's slogans still decorated the walls. A ripe odor of sweat, strong perfume and sex was overpowering. The dark-haired woman with deep brown skin and a curious look was peeking out from under the blankets in Merc's bed. When she saw Veronica, she wiggled from the covers, slipped a dress over her head, grabbed her sandals and ran out the back.

Veronica watched her without a word. Stunned, she turned to Merc. "Hijole. I am here at the wrong time." Veronica wouldn't make eye contact with him.

"She's my house cleaner."

"House cleaner my ass." Veronica was not going to let this get to her. But she was quick to anger. "Bet it's the well-traveled Magdalena."

Merc shrugged. "You seem to know a lot about me."

"Our research team at the agency gave me a dossier on you. We knew about your friends in the village. It's pretty common knowledge that you also had a professional interest in everybody's plaything Maggie."

Merc nodded. "So, what can I say?"

"Don't say anything. I can't believe this. I mean you swore to me you respected Mexican women. You…who should be aware of social issues and you are shacked up with a…a…"

"A prostitute?"

Veronica was ratcheting up. She poked her finger at his chest. "Yes, you. You who are so worried about polluting the air and the ground. You are polluting your personal world, my culture and our friendship."

"Our friendship?"

"Well, something that might have been. You intrigued me. I must have been loca."

Merc sighed. "Sorry you feel that way."

"Why, Merc. Why would you do this? You are a handsome guy. You have a chance to hook up with single women. Find love in a lasting social relationship."

"Well. I have multiple ex-wives. And, as a French philosopher once said, at this age we don't love, we just please each other."

"No, you need love. And you could have had the right woman. I mean…a smart woman who has a salary. Who goes to the gym and takes care of herself." She banged her fist on her taut stomach. "But, no. You take the fucking easy way. This…this paying for sex."

Merc sucked in an audible breath and stared her down. "Really, I don't pay for sex. I pay to avoid relationships built around sex. These Sunday nights are a good part of my spending." Merc began to pick up clothes.

"Look. I came here with some exciting news. But I'm not sure I want to tell you now. Your friend will probably spread it around the village like she spreads her knees for pesos."

"I don't have to tell her anything. What's the news?"

Veronica glanced around the room and frowned. "This place is a mess."

"Some vandals trashed my house yesterday."

"Well, it smells awful in here. Horrible perfume. And don't blame that on the vandals. *Fea*—ugh. I don't really want to be in this room. Let's talk on the patio. But before we do, shouldn't you see to your little hooker?"

Merc stepped outside for a moment and looked around. There was no sign of Maggie. "She seems to be gone. I'll get coffee."

Veronica sat on a beat-up plastic chair and stared at the morning sky. Noisy gulls squawked as they circled above the palapa. Aromas of seaweed and fish flooded the patio. The overwhelming peace at Merc's place cooled Veronica's ire for the moment.

Merc shambled out with coffee and handed her a cup.

"Thanks." She took a sip, and spit it out. "Ugh. This is bitter." Then she leaned over closer to him. "This morning is so calm. This place is easy to love. Merc, I have to tell you something that is confidential. You cannot tell anyone. Here goes."

"Okay."

"Our office has been studying the Bat-Mex plant. And, after all the scrutiny, we concluded there was little or no pollution. This baffled us. But then we joined forces with the other agencies and we found that there wasn't much pollution because, guess what, they really weren't processing that many batteries. In fact, they only handled one-tenth the batteries they said they were doing. What do you make of that?"

"I don't know."

"Come on. Guess what was going on."

"No. You know, I don't want to get mixed up in anything."

"Well, yes, you would be wise to keep out of it. Not that you weren't messing with it by loving it up with this perfumed whore. Crap. I can't believe it. What is my problem?" Veronica sat silent for a moment. "Relationships aren't fucking worth it, are they?" She looked at him with a wan smile. "I have an ex-mate too and I enjoy sex but I don't go around hiring gigolos." She fumed and then settled down. "Well, I'll only tell you this. You will soon be offered a new place to live."

"Hope it's not jail."

"I would approve of that but no, it's in Refugio."

Merc had his own news. "I'll tell you what I've heard yesterday. Rumors in the village say the new ejido managers are going to expand the plant or build condos on the sandspit."

"Yes. As far as I know, it is going to happen."

"So the factory will close and the shit will be flying here. I will be a hated man."

"You already have a bad rep. When I was here last, Gaby and I became friends. She talked you up, saying you were exciting and fun. This time, she couldn't say enough bad things about you."

"If the Señora is down on me…I am really in trouble."

"Not as much as you think. And you can't tell a soul. Even Gabriela. There is talk the government will dissolve Bat-Mex and another company will take over and continue to run the battery plant. That's our victory and it all began with you, Merc. You and your story about how you smuggled your wood into Mexico."

"You mean, by making a box out of the wood and putting junk in it?"

"That's it. That's how we got onto them. They weren't shipping out old battery cases, but they were forming their contraband into the shape of used battery case parts. It was truly inventive. We found a whole shipment on a truck headed to Mexicali. There was more contraband on that crashed plane. That did it. And do you want to know what was in those old cases?"

"No. Instead, tell me how soon will the other company move in?"

"Very soon. Maybe next week. But that's super confidential. Once again, I have to swear you to secrecy. On your honor. And that's not all. There soon will be a big army push against the cartel."

"Do you know when?"

"Just soon. I'm not sure exactly."

"So, until the village finds out about the takeover, the workers will think they are out of a job and I will be pig shit to the local folks."

"Probably."

Finally, Merc was warming to this attractive scientist. She had been hinting about friendship. Long ago, when she first stepped off the Flying Medics plane, he had fanaticized about connecting with her. Physically. Moments ago, she said she enjoyed sex. Was there still a chance? "Do you want some breakfast?"

"I would have loved to...but no. Not after meeting your overnight friend. No, I don't want to eat with someone like you who cares so little for himself."

Merc sensed this was hopeless. He stood up. "Well, thanks for judging me. It's not the first time that has happened and won't be the last. Still, I appreciate the heads up on the factory. Where are you off to now?"

"I've got a meeting in San Felipe and then I drive back to Mexicali and fly back to the capitol. And promise me again, Merc, that you won't tell Gabriela or anyone about this."

"Why would I?"

"I can see that you still have a few brain cells left even if the others haven't been corrupted by the dirty sex that you so carelessly indulge in. Better get yourself checked for diseases."

Veronica walked to the front of the house and grabbed her purse. She returned to face Merc, who was standing by his back door gazing out at the Sea of Cortez.

"You are such a stupid man. And a paradox—like any man. A fighter against ruining the environment but can't keep his pants on. No wonder you're living in this isolated shithole."

"Sorry. You didn't think it was a shithole five minutes ago."

"Not the place, Merc. I'm talking about your life. I mean I drove all the way down here. I guess I am more stupid than you. Goodbye, Merc."

Merc watched as Veronica started her rental car. It sat for minutes in the driveway with the engine idling before she shut off the motor and strode back to where Merc stood.

"Do I get a second chance?" asked Merc.

Veronica wasn't listening. She had fire in her eyes. "It just occurred to me. You must have known I was coming. Tell me the truth."

"No. I never guessed you would show up here."

"Was this a setup? Did you arrange for your friend to be here?"

"No. She's always here on the first Sunday of the month. That's when I get my check."

"You sure no one told you I was coming."

"If someone told me, why would I have her here?"

A furious look spread across here face. "Ah, yes. Now I can pretty much guess. I thought Gaby was straight with me when she said you love surprises in the morning. What a two-faced, double-dealing bitch that woman is."

Veronica spun on her heels, then stopped and looked back. "You really aren't any prize, you know. Just another lame excuse. You're a dick." She slammed the door on her rental and roared out of the driveway, spitting back a trail of rocks and sandy dust.

Merc thought for a long time about clever responses to that last remark. Couldn't come up with anything. Then, he looked around once more for Maggie but decided she must have hoofed it back to Refugio.

He sat down in a hammock under his palapa to ponder the loose ends. There was no hope for a hook-up with the hot-tempered Veronica. But that was okay. Maybe he really didn't trust her. After all, what was this hot-shot environmental scientist doing mixed up in the big cartel investigation? And what did she know that she didn't tell him?

Still, I am in shit city, thought Merc. *The Señora is down on me. The village doesn't know what I know and will hate me. The drug agents are swarming the town. The army may make dangerous moves against the cartel. Maybe the cartel will come looking for me.*

There was only one thing to do. Go fishing. Merc decided to put the anxieties aside for the moment and fire up the *Outta Here*. The tide was in and he would spend the afternoon relaxing on the Sea of Cortez. He knew tomorrow would be the all-consuming event. Everyone on the sandspit was getting ready for a blowout party.

31

Dueling Fiestas

The next morning, Merc stayed away from Playa
Refugio, choosing instead to scrub off the walls and
straighten out his place. He opened both doors and
a sea breeze cleaned out the stale odors. It was time
to organize his few possessions—a painful task. In the
end, he sorted it down to four cartons of personal stuff—
photos, files and clothes—a quantity that would fit in the
pickup's toolbox. Assuming all the rumors were true and
that the ejido might eventually tear down his house and
kick him off the sandspit, he would abandon the rest to
the scavengers or the bulldozers. Travel light was going to
be the mantra.

In late afternoon, Merc headed for his outdoor shower. It was the Fourth of July—Ruby's birthday—and the
sandspit ratas, plus a few other ex-pat seasonal residents,
a pair of confused Australian surfers and some French visitors had reserved a celebratory table on the patio at El
Parador for an all-out fiesta.

RJ showed up as Merc finished dressing. They both retreated to the shade of the palapa on the patio, where they spent time drinking beers and waiting for Doc, Ruby and Shay.

"RJ, you might want to know."

"And that is."

"That jerk who came through earlier asking about religious cults, the one who said he is a fisherman and doesn't know anything about fish, is back."

"Did he talk to you again?"

"No. But he asked Gaby some questions? She said the pendejo was looking for former ministers. She told him nothing."

"Thanks. That's a good heads up. They might be closing in."

"So get smart. Stop acting like an ex-minister."

"Okay. Good idea. But I'm not going to worry about this tonight."

When everyone had assembled by his door, Merc grabbed his boombox and enough CDs for a drunken night of revelry. Tonight's birthday celebration was going to be a momentous affair. After all, how often did Ruby turn 50? Besides, the way things were going, this might be a final blowout for what was left of the Punta Gringa gang.

They all piled into Shay's old rusty Oldsmobile. The slightly lubricated group sang two versions of *Happy Birthday* to Ruby as they bounced down the dirt road toward Playa Refugio. The sandspit clique always used the Parador patio for their parties because the restaurant tolerated loud yelling, off-key singing and ear-blistering music, not to mention the deranged dancing. Other patrons had two choices—get swept up into the group's jovial revelry or pack up and go home.

But tonight would be even more chaotic. When the Gringans arrived, they found wooden signs detouring traffic around the block that fronted the El Parador's patio. It was the feast day of La Señora del Refugio and the date for the ejido's annual public street barbecue and party. Tables were spread out across the closed roadway and an oil drum cooker was smoking, its grill covered with fish filets and hunks of steak. Two large plastic trashcans held ice, beer and sodas. Thirty to forty people stood around eating from paper plates. ChuChu Acosta and Alan the Croatian were playing amateur ranchera music through the amplifier.

Dueling fiestas. It was going to be one noisy night. The partygoers for Ruby began draining pitchers of margaritas and devouring El Parador's savory taquitos and salsas. Ex-pats who lived north of town joined in. Before long, Ismael brought out salads, roasted meats and chicken, along with tortillas and frijoles. The El Parador was entering jolly party mode.

Both celebrations got livelier. The night roared with cheer. When the gringos had consumed most of their food and polished off their fifth pitcher of margaritas, it was time for Ruby's birthday cake. Ismael went to the curb and made an impassioned speech to the partygoers in the street, many who wandered over and gathered around Ruby.

As the crowd waited, Shay appeared with a cake with 50 candles. There was an explosion of applause and the mostly drunken crowd began two rounds of *Happy Birthday*. Ruby embraced Shay and both began to cry. The singers also began a slow and intoxicated version of *Las Mananitas*, the Mexican birthday song. Presents appeared and Ruby opened them to cheers.

While the sandspit gang continued to party on the patio, the ejido celebrants drifted back to the street. The Galindo Family band, with two amplified guitars, a bass, a trumpet and drums, had taken the stage and began playing a slightly off-key blend of Mexican favorites and old rock and roll. The younger couples got up to dance and brought their kids out too.

Ruby's friends went through margarita pitchers number six and seven and were reaching the edge of hysterics. Ruby, Doc and Shay stumbled out to dance in the street. Merc sat with RJ and the other ex-pat couples, loudly discussing the annoyances caused by the latest searches of beachfront shacks.

Then, the little patio gathering went silent. Merc slowly looked up. The Señora was standing across the table, this time without her trademark baseball cap and dark glasses. Her hair was down and it was the first time Merc had ever seen her in a dress.

"Merc. It's time. It's time to prove you can dance. Quieres bailar—do you want to dance? You once told me you danced like el Diablo."

Merc was shocked. All eyes were on him. Would he?

"No, I…uh."

The two French couples urged him on. RJ was in hysterics—he almost threw up he laughed so hard. "Baile, Merc. Baile—dance—with the scorpion. Someone up there will help."

Gaby urged him on. "Come on, Merc. If RJ is right, you'll have Jesus on your side."

"Sure. I'd love to." And Merc slowly rose, raised his eyes skyward as if asking for divine help, tucked in his shirt, and walked Gaby back to the street. He took her hand and held it. This touch seemed necessary, perfunctory, and almost mechanical; but when he put his other hand on her back, it spoke too much of intimacy. She felt solid, sweaty, and alive. How tightly should be hold her? He was getting lost in her perfume and his fourth margarita. The music tempo slowed and they were face-to-face. Gaby smiled.

She has to have some reason for this. She has to. "I must admit. This is a helluva surprise," said Merc.

"Why, Merc? You are a *guapo*—handsome—man and I am a lovely unemployed single woman with two daughters in college."

"That's all true…"

"So, this could be the start of something beautiful."

"We'll see. I think this dance is where I hear some bad news about the ejido."

"There's no good news. I have been officially replaced."

"I'm sorry to hear that."

"But let's not talk about it yet."

"We could talk about a recent morning surprise."

"I take it you were shocked to see a visitor."

"As I saw it, someone in the village suggested this visitor arrive unannounced at my door," said Merc.

"Wasn't that a great move? Everyone in the village

knows where Maggie goes on the first Sunday night of the month. And, I had become very tired of that uptight know-it-all bitch scientist from Mexico City."

"She said you were down on me."

"Don't believe everything a Chilanga says."

The two danced slowly. Up until now, Merc had thought of Gaby as a powerful overlord with a whipsmart mind. Now, her body was pressing up against his. Parallel universes moving in sync. In a million years, he never imagined this would be happening. He moved her back a bit and stared at her.

Gaby caught his look. "Merc. I am flattered you are giving me the once over."

"I was not."

"Yes you were. A woman knows. You are thinking—even though she is forty-five, with a little bit of fat here and there, I wonder what she is like as a lover?"

Merc only shrugged. He grinned. Yes, he was feeling the attraction but after all, he was shitfaced. Buzzed. *Borracho*—drunk. The music shifted to an even slower song. Many younger couples sat down or chased their children. Merc and Gaby continued to dance. His mind was on its side. Was this a beginning of something he had religiously avoided? He already had two ex-wives. This tough, powerful woman that RJ called a force of nature—why was she moving on him? He knew very little about her. To add to his confusion, he worried why he was worrying about all this.

"So, my friend. How's it going?" asked Gaby.

"Ruby's having a great birthday. We're going to shoot off some fireworks later. It's America's Independence Day.

Tonight's going very well. Very well, thank you. What's the news about the battery plant?"

"Well, Merc. Alex and his supporters are making the factory his first action as ejido president. They are thinking the plant should be three times its size. They need more room for more factory buildings, more storage outbuildings and parking. Perhaps condos too."

Merc thought for a moment. "If they do this, how long will the planning take?"

"There is no planning. I think it's ready to go now. I think Alex plans to move our sandspit renters to the north of town. It could happen in a week."

"But I don't want to live north of town. It's windy there. Ugly. You can't launch a boat from the beach. We signed a lease. The ejido should honor..." Merc was confused by the margaritas and Gaby's attention.

Gaby put her finger to his lips. "Merc, these are younger people. They don't want my generation's promises. I only told you this to warn you. So enjoy this moment."

Merc drew her closer. Her hair sparkled with red highlights and streaks of gray and was redolent of a hundred roses. Tiny wrinkles and artfully shaped brows framed her reddish brown eyes.

They stared at each other. He couldn't believe he was this close and concerned about her troubles. "What will you do? Will you stay in the village?"

She grinned. "I'm going to leave Refugio. Probably within a week. I'll go first to San Felipe and then to the Pacific coast. My sister has a house in Playa Descanso south of Rosarita. It's beautiful."

"You are kidding. Gaby, your leaving now is a tragedy."

Gaby stopped their slow dance. Her eyes locked on him. "Merc. You said my name. Am I no longer la Señora? That's a first step. And tell me. Why a tragedy? Why Merc?"

Merc didn't want to answer truthfully. He was surprised he had called her Gaby. His thoughts echoed off the inside of his skull in a margarita fog. "Would you like, Gaby, to have a drink before you go?"

She laughed. "What a line? Yes, of course I would, Merc. I never thought you'd ask. But I hoped you would. You know we can't do it in this village. The tongues would roar. We'd have to go up to San Felipe, where I have a casita. Or," and she smiled broadly, "maybe we could save that drink for my new patio in Descanso and watch the sunset over the Pacific."

Merc pulled her tighter—the tequila had kicked in big-time. He was light-headed. Everything was a daze. Her body had stirred feelings and her skin looked creamy and inviting. This is absurd. He moved his head down and pushed her hair to the side, struggling at the same time to nudge a lingering kiss on her neck, just below her ear. She drew her head away and smiled. "Hey, cowboy, take it easy. Slow down."

"Oops," was all he could say. Thinking was very difficult. Both stood rock still. She stared at him and tightened the grip on his hand.

"This is all very sudden. Gaby, I…I'd better go help pay for this fiesta." Merc excused himself, flashed a shit-eating grin and slowly backed away, stumbling to the party table on the Parador patio. The raucous music was banging inside his head. When he finally reached the table, RJ stood up and applauded wildly. Merc sat down hard. His folding chair fell over backward and he spilled onto the ground. Everyone laughed.

RJ and Doc were clearly drunk and trying to divvy up the check. Merc joined them, but was of little help. They all started throwing pesos onto the table, the pile growing until Ismael nodded affirmatively. When it was done, the next discussion began about who was the least drunk and would eventually drive the old station wagon back to Gringa. Because they figured everybody from the sandspit was at the fiesta, and there would be little or no traffic on the road, the driver only had to be someone who could point the car in the right direction, keep it from rolling off the shoulder into a ditch and put the brakes on when they got there.

32

The House of Bones

Enrique had been watching the raucous fiestas from the back of the crowd. The savory aroma of the barbecued chicken tormented him. The promise of cold beers on ice taunted him. He'd love to be smoking a joint right now and dancing. But he didn't dare. He understood, oh so well, that he was a known buffoon in this village. Everyone could recognize his face and connect him to his well-publicized indiscretion. Staying anonymous was the best path now.

And yet, this posed a dilemma. It was clear that if he didn't turn up some important clues soon, advance the intel on the drone attacks, that his career at Border Protection might be over. Next week he could be working at a hardware outlet in Yuma hawking lawn sprinklers.

The evidence had to be in Punta Gringa. The community of strays and recluses living on the sandspit struck him as a suspicious lot. If the Gringans weren't directly involved with the cartel's smuggling and counter drone program, they had to have brushed up against these criminals at some point.

So, it was time to act. While the sandspitters were still drunk and dancing, he could set out for the deserted Punta Gringa. There he might have an hour or so to rummage unmolested through any of the shacks.

Even in the dark, it was a sweaty two-mile hike. When he arrived, the place was eerily quiet; the entire population really was at the party.

His next step was outside regulations. This was a path he never thought he'd take. Breaking into houses. El Aguila was to become a rogue agent.

Castillo threaded his way among the deserted trailers and mobile homes, heading for his first objective—the shack with a hand-written sign advertising fiberglass repair. The front door was locked, but a side window slid open and he crawled in.

He turned on a miniature flashlight. What a mess. Clothes seemed to be thrown everywhere and the kitchen table was piled with rocks. Bleached cattle skulls hung from the walls. Old mining equipment was stacked in the corner. He began to go through papers spread out on a cluttered desk. He thought this might be Doc's house, but there were no signs of that. In fact, he hadn't ever learned Doc's name. Only Doc. Not having a background dossier made Enrique uneasy. Still, this was a creepy house. *What kind of freak lives here? Skulls? This is weird.*

He paused. Nothing in the house but old equipment and bones. That was it. A few photographs. Enrique pocketed a group shot of the Gringa crowd. But no guns. No pictures of drones. A few joints in an ashtray but no sign of serious drugs. No obvious clues at all. He carefully replaced everything he touched, cautious not to leave any sign he was there. Then he crawled back out the window and shut it.

Behind this building was a padlocked shed. Through a slit in the walls he could see a workbench covered with car repair tools. A trolling outboard motor sat on another worktable. Seemed innocent enough. Crouching low, he swiftly moved through the dark to the next building on the sandspit, a burned-out mobile home.

Enrique's heart was racing. The break-in, though it yielded nothing, was the slippery slope into illegal undercover tactics. Right now, he needed time to think. Hunched down inside the fire-blackened trailer, he inflated his surveillance arena cushion, chewed an energy bar and prepared for the long haul.

There was little chance to relax. Two men drove a pickup down the hill, passed by the abandoned mobile home where Enrique was hiding and stopped at the last house on the sandspit. They jumped out yelling and laughing loudly, then grabbed portable gas tanks from the truck bed. In the headlights, he could see them dousing the outside wall with what appeared to be gasoline, setting a spark to it and crazily driving off down a dark sandy desert road. The flames took off and within minutes, the structure was an inferno.

What should he do? Put out the blaze? That would give away his position. Before he could react, a car's lights appeared on the grade weaving back and forth. Over the crackle of the fire, he could hear singing and yelling. The sandspit community of five was returning from the drunken birthday party. Everyone was packed into Shay's old station wagon with the windows down and RJ driving.

Behind him, the burning house began to explode. Thunderous blasts came one after the other. Flaming embers shot hundreds of feet into the air.

Everyone in the station wagon saw it.

"Well somebody is setting off fireworks," observed the completely drunken Doc.

Shay was sloshed but she stared hard at the inferno. "It's not fireworks, guys. It's...it's...it's Taras Blubber's old house." And Shay laughed hysterically.

Orange flames were roaring, lighting up the desert as if it was noon. Wind gusts whipped embers into the nearby ironwood brush, which caught fire and burned brightly, illuminating more of the sandspit.

RJ drove right past Enrique's hiding place and pulled up at the edge of the flames. Everyone got out.

"Hey. Great fireworks. Anybody got marshmallows?" said Doc.

"What do you think we should do?" asked Merc.

RJ laughed. "Let's all sit and watch it burn. It'll be out in about ten minutes and as long as it doesn't spread to anything, it's better than a few bottle rockets."

The drunken sandspit ratas snagged chairs from RJ's trailer and set them up in a perimeter around the flames. Shay came back with a cold six-pack of Pacificos.

Enrique guessed the Punta Gringans were now 30 yards away, sitting in a line with their backs to him, facing the fire. He worried they might find him hiding out in the mobile home wreck and blame him for the arson. He had to take a chance to get the hell out of there. Grabbing his backpack, he slipped around the back and took off running away from the fire and into the darkness.

RJ sensed a noise and turned. "Hey, back there. By Eliot's house." RJ pointed to a shadowy figure sprinting from the burned out mobile home next to Eliot's. The runner was now over a hundred yards away and disappearing into the night. *Goddam vandals,* Merc thought. *Probably from the ejido's new bosses. Lucky he didn't hit any of our places.*

Dashing through the coal black night was reckless. Heading up the grade beside the road, Enrique stumbled, twisting his ankle and stabbing his hand into a low-growing cactus as he hit the dirt. Spines punctured the heel of his palm. It hurt like hell. But he got up and ran again, finally reaching his comfortable surveillance post in the rocks overlooking Punta Gringa. He wasn't sure whether the returning gringos had recognized him. The first aid kit had tweezers and he painfully pulled each thorn from his skin, before spilling bottled water over the puncture wounds. Finally, he spread on disinfectant and wrapped it in an awkward bandage.

What now? The more he thought about it, the more he had regrets about his hasty search at the fiberglass repair house. He had been nervous. It was his first break-in, so there were obvious places he had overlooked, cupboards and cabinets he didn't open. These had been a newbie agent's mistakes.

The answers had to be in that spooky shack with the cattle skulls. He still had his Glock. Dawn tomorrow would be the moment for the eagle to do what El Toro probably did a hundred times—get nasty with the bad guys. Sharpen his talons. Attack at dawn. Hit them while they slept. Time to put the hammer down.

33

Tied Up Again

The harsh cries from seagulls and the morning glow spreading across the Sea of Cortez intruded on Enrique's anxiety dreams. He had been caught breaking into a house and now was being dragged by goats through Punta Gringa's sandy streets while the laughing residents threw garbage at him. La Gringa was standing by the side, holding a glass jar of red ants, beaming contemptuously and beckoning to him with her finger.

Spending the night on rocks had been torture. Muscles get twisted and legs cramped. A few yoga stretches unloosened the kinks in his shoulders but the ankle was still tender and the right hand swollen, oozing pus from underneath the bandage. He unpacked his Glock and tried gripping it in his left hand. It felt firm and steady. At the pistol range, he had learned to shoot with either hand, being ready for just such a situation.

Finishing off two strawberry-flavored yogurt energy bars, Enrique slipped out of the rocky observation point and crept down the hillside into Punta Gringa. This was his moment to be a hard ass. The target once again was the house with the fiberglass repair sign. There were no vehicles outside—a solid omen it might be vacant.

He went to the door and silently forced it open. The dim light revealed a sleeping figure in the bed, snoring loudly. The Glock came out, trained on the body.

"U.S. federal border agent. Don't move. Don't move or I'll shoot."

The form in the bed turned over. The hair reminded him of that dark-skinned woman who had snubbed him at the café in Playa Refugio.

"What? What?" Shay tried to pry her eyes open. Was this another morning after nightmare? Her head was splitting. It throbbed from the overdose of birthday party margaritas. One eyelid remained stuck shut. Through the other, she saw a blurred form.

"Don't move. Slowly stand and put your hands up."

She could see the blunt end of a semi-automatic pistol pointed at her. Horribly hung over, she meekly obeyed, unsteadily climbing out of bed and standing there, arms dangling at her side. She wasn't wearing a stitch.

"Put your hands up. I told you to put them up."

"I'm too tired. Do I have to?"

"Put them fucking up," he screamed. And she did.

Enrique paused for a long time and stared. She was tiny, bony, deep brown and very naked. He could see tattoos on her arms and below her waist. She was wearing a silver bicep bracelet, a cobra with shining ruby eyes. The short cut black hair was rumpled and stuck straight up. The stuffiness in the airless room reminded him of those mornings after his romps with Sylvia. Standing there now was a new Ofelia, the Narco Queen. Only this time, the gun was real.

Enrique demanded answers. "Who are you? Why are you here? Where's the person who owns this house?"

"Who are you looking for?" said the woman sleepily. She yawned repeatedly. "Do you mind if I get some water. Gaach. My mouth tastes like chalk. And can I put my hands down now?"

"No, don't move." Castillo thought about Doc. "Doc. I'm looking for Doc."

"Doc who? Doc doesn't live here." Finally Shay managed to open the second eye. She focused on the gunman. "Oh, it's our agent friend. I bet you don't know. You don't even know who you are looking for?"

"What the hell are you doing here? Why don't you put a robe on?"

"I was here to water plants. When the owner's out of town, I sleep in this bed. It's comfortable. And I like to sleep naked." She passed her hand across her body as if demonstrating a product. "Do you like what you see?"

"Is he coming back?"

"Don't know. The owner will be gone for a while."

"Do you know where he is? What's his name?"

"I'm not going to tell you. But I know your name. You're the agent who they call the whacker. You are the peeping Tom. Everybody knows that. You are Enrique Castillo, son of the greatest drug agent ever."

"Don't give me shit. Where is the guy who lives here?"

Shay swayed. She needed a glass of water. Her head

throbbed. "Don't know, mister agent Whacker. Off suck-
ing the blood out of cattle so he can bleach their skulls.
No one knows where the owner goes. The owner tells us
how long it will be and then just goes. Look, I need water
and an aspirin. I feel sick. I might throw up."

Castillo was still staring at the naked Shay. He was
ambivalent about where to take this.

This gave her an advantage. "Are you getting excited
by my body? Is it something you want? Like the other
woman you saw and you started whacking off? How about
my breasts? Very tiny, aren't they. Do you like them bigger?" And she started to rub her hands on her breasts.

Enrique retreated to training. He would use textbook
arrest procedure. "You'll have to turn around. I've got to
search you."

Shay laughed in his face and did a dance step as she
turned, placing her hand on one butt cheek. "Do you want
to do a cavity search, oh mighty agent?"

Castillo paused. He took a deep breath. He had to
conduct himself as if she had a gun somewhere, maybe
in the bed. "Move to your left a bit, over by the wood
stove. Stand by those bones. But move slowly." Castillo
waved his pistol toward the skulls. "I have to search for
hidden weapons."

Shay relaxed. Her power to befuddle the agent was
growing. "It's Enrique, right? Come closer to me, Enrique.
I can feel your warmth. I can take care of your needs."
Shay began to moan sarcastically.

Enrique's mouth was dry. Once more, long ignored
forces made their presence felt. He was getting sexually
excited. This wasn't working out like they taught in agent

training. Moving slowly toward the bed, he carried the gun in his left hand and reached out with the right to push Shay from his path. He touched her hip and a pain from the cactus wound shot up his arm, startling him. The Glock went off with a thunderous bang, blowing a hole in the wall. "Son of a bitch," he said.

Shay screamed and fell backward by the cattle skulls. Enrique motioned for her to get back up. When she was standing again, he slowly moved past her. At the bed, he threw back the covers. Nothing there. He began to reach across the mattress for a bulky bag on the bed strand when he heard a footstep. He turned just in time to see a cattle skull crashing down on his head.

—∿—

Castillo came to when water splashed on his face. He was tied to a chair. Shay was dressed and standing over him holding a Colt .45 semi-automatic in both hands. The barrel was less than a foot from his face. Her expression was particularly grim and her body was shaking. "I should just shoot your fat face and bury your body in the dirt."

A fearful look spread across the agent's face.

"Whoa, what's going on?" Castillo said.

"Got you again, you sex pervert," said Shay. "I knew these skulls had some use."

Castillo's head throbbed. Blood was caked on his face from a cut on his forehead. A man sat in the background. He turned woozily toward him. "And who are you?" he asked. "Do you live here?"

"Couldn't say for sure," Merc answered. "I did hear a shot, so I came to see what was going on."

"Well, I am Agent Enrique Castillo. U.S. Customs and Border Protection and I want you to release me."

"Fat chance, agent pervert." Merc said. "We caught you breaking into a house out here. We caught you touching our women and shooting holes in the walls."

Shay was frothing. She moved the barrel closer to his face. "And, agent Castillo, you are in Mexico. No frigging way can you come down here to stick a gun in my face. Or point it at my naked body. Or touch me. You touched me. Now I'm thinking of calling the San Felipe police."

She picked up his pistol and showed it to him. "While you were unconscious, I unloaded your Glock. Then I found your crappy backpack outside and the extra ammo." She dumped four mangled ammunition magazines on the floor. "So I smashed them with a hammer and buried the ammo. So your gun, like you, you asshole, is useless." Shay screamed at Enrique, "Now watch me. Watch this, asshole. I am going to put this worthless gun back in your backpack." And she did.

Merc was smiling. "I read *Steel Bull in the Desert.* Your father sounded like a decent man. Now, you appear to be the embarrassing family disgrace. Why in god's name did you come back into Punta Gringa after your first humiliating capture."

"I can't…"

"Well, you must have had a reason."

"Government business."

"Well, then, you know, unless you tell us, you will be tied up for a long time."

Castillo thought it over. "Okay. I need to talk to the person who repairs fiberglass."

"At gunpoint. By rousting someone with a hangover. Helluva friendly way to chat," said Merc. "And what do you want from this person?"

"It's part of an ongoing investigation. I can't tell you."

"Well. I'll surprise you. I'll answer your questions. What if there is someone in Punta Gringa who repairs boats and fiberglass panels?"

"Who does he do jobs for?"

"Whoever pulls in with a boat."

Merc leaned over to Castillo "Okay, Agent El Fuckup, what else do you want to know?"

"Did he ever repair any small fiberglass airplanes?"

"Don't know."

"Did he ever have any dealings with a Cuban?"

"Yeah. There was a guy in Refugio who spoke with a strange accent. I think it was Caribbean or Cuban."

Enrique was not surprised. The Cuban was on the agency's cartel radar. "Damn. That's good. That's what I need to know. Where I can find this Cuban?"

"Don't know. Maybe Puertecitos. He said he lived in Puertecitos. He seemed like a pleasant guy." Merc was lying.

"Thanks, that's what I need to know. Can you let me go?"

"Yeah. Right. You stormed into a house where someone was sleeping. You stuck a gun in a woman's face. A loaded gun. You admired her naked body and her breasts and fondled her bare hip. You shot a hole in the wall with your Glock. You are a bit crazy, a bit over the top. A real pervert."

"So I'm going to stay here for a while?"

"Actually no. I have a plan. Maybe we'll drop you off at the curandera's place. Everyone in Refugio heard she had a good solution for your schoolboy peeping tendencies—ants and goat shit." Merc chuckled.

"No, please don't do that."

"Why shouldn't we?"

"If she does the ants on the feet thing, and my boss hears of it, I'll lose my job."

"And we're better off because you have this job?"

"I am a very competent federal agent."

Shay waved her pistol around. "Stop this bullshit. Let's take him to Athena."

"No. Better idea. We'll tie him up and at night, I'll drive him to San Felipe. I'll leave him at the deserted Pemex gas station that is just at this end of town, and call the police. I'll tell them he was peeping at naked women again. The police down here understand knife fights, gunfights, burglary, arson, car theft, bar brawls, cockfights, dogfights, vandalism, smuggling, drugs and lots of things. But they really don't like perverts who prey on women. And they are willing to look the other way while the locals beat the crap out of them."

Castillo was mortified. "Please don't do that. Don't hand me over to the local police."

Merc smiled. He looked at Shay. "Okay. Okay. Better idea. We'll call his office and tell them what he did and that we hit him with a skull and where to find their agent."

Shay turned toward Castillo. "And if I ever catch you snooping around the women in Punta Gringa again, I will cut your cojones off."

Merc grinned. "I think the woman seems righteously

pissed off. Have you asked her out for a drink? Or apologized for scaring the shit out of her?"

Castillo looked up at Shay. "Sorry. It was a mistake."

Shay picked up another skull and swung it, smacking Enrique on the shoulder. Merc took it away from her.

"So, agent Whacker, you are going to take a little trip in my pickup. The route covers rough roads, because we have to avoid the checkpoints. But I'll get you there and call your office. Now, we have to remove your clothes down to your underwear and tie you up. And if you so much as try to resist, I will let my enraged friend shoot you in the balls."

They stripped Enrique to his boxers. Shay laughed when she saw the aborted tattoo on his back. "It looks like a chicken massaging a banana." Then they encircled him with duct tape. He knew his colleagues in Yuma would laugh themselves silly over this one. Once more the son had disgraced his father's legend. El Toro must have been turning over in his grave.

34

The Prodigal

"You can pick up your agent at the abandoned Pemex on the big curve south of San Felipe. He got a naked woman out of bed at gunpoint, fondled her hip and then fired a round through a wall. Finally, he was trying to get close to her when she hit him on the head with a cattle skull."

The Captain listened to a recording of the message. He ordered the two San Felipe U.S. Border Protection agents to go look for Castillo. They rushed to the boarded-up gas station on curve out of town. Fearing an ambush, they drew their guns and stepped through piles of garbage and trash in a room-by-room search. In an upstairs office, the pair found fellow agent Enrique Castillo in his underwear, bound with duct tape and sitting against a wall. He had spent the early morning hours in the cold, dank room that stunk of urine. His Glock pistol was in the middle of the floor, surrounded by ammunition magazines that had been crushed.

The rescuers called the Yuma office.

"Captain Dolan. We found our AWOL agent. The one with the chicken holding the banana tattoo. He's chilled but fine. Nearly naked but most of his clothes and equipment were in a pile next to him."

"Let me speak to him."

The agent handed the phone to Enrique, who had been untied and was wrapped in a blanket.

"Captain, I can explain everything."

"I'm sure you can, Castillo."

"I want you to know I think I've found the key to the case. I am very close to solving it."

"Agent Castillo, the only key you might need is to the brig at the local Marine Corps Air Station in Yuma."

"No, sir. I mean that I think I know where the cartel is controlling the anti-drones from."

"Well, here's what you should know. We used a Skyfire missile and shot down one of their motherships as it slid in above the Predator. That's the good news. Unfortunately, the ordinance in the Skyfire obliterated the cartel's drone, so we didn't get anything to work with."

"Great. Captain, that's great. But I think I know where their ops center is. It's an area that I spent a lot of time in when I was a field agent. Let me take the San Felipe team to the location today."

"Well, show agents Marquez and Sanchez on the map but then you'll have to come back here."

"I'll come back but first I'd better go into the field to show these guys."

"Castillo. Our anonymous tipster who told us where to find you also mentioned that you had another run in

with a naked woman. The caller said you broke into a
sleeping woman's house, wanted to search her while she
was naked, made her stand there without clothes before
you pawed her, then fired a shot through the wall. Is that
correct?"

"Yeah, that's it."

"I'm getting real tired of this crap. This is your second report of a flagrant sexual harassment during an official search. Castillo, what the fuck were you thinking?
Can't you stay away from naked women?"

"Well, she had been in bed."

"Why not have her put some clothes on?"

"Well, sir, there wasn't time. I didn't paw her. I just
pushed her a little. She might have had a weapon in the
bed. I had to search it before I could do the rest of the
house. I was looking for the fiberglass connection with the
Cuban and the cartel."

"Like you searched the woman sunbathing on the
sailboat. Or the woman in the shower?"

"Well, Iris on the sailboat had a gun."

"The caller said you were trying to get close to her
when she finally knocked you unconscious by smacking
that thick cabeza of yours with a cattle skull."

"I guess that is what happened. But I'd like to go
back to that house again. I feel in my bones that it is
involved."

"And why would your bones help us? Did you find
anything the first time?"

"Not really. Only that it is definitely where the fiberglass guy lives. I think I spoke to him. He said he'd met
the Cuban, who might be living in Puertecitos. Still, I

think I should go back to that house at Punta Gringa."

"Castillo, you aren't going back to Punta Gringa. Now, go to the safe house in San Felipe, debrief the other agents on your finds and then we'll bring you back to Yuma."

"Okay, sir."

Castillo sat in the black Suburban for the short ride to the San Felipe Ops center. Once there, he took a shower and watched television. When the other agents left to check with the Mexican counterparts, Enrique set about preparing for his next outing.

———

Two hours later, the San Felipe agents were back at the safe house. Enrique had been busy, locating new magazines for the Glock pistol, loading them and stuffing a backpack with clean clothes. He briefed his colleagues about the maze in the Sal Si Puedes Canyon, but the two were unfamiliar with the area and were reluctant to set out into the hot, arid, and unforgiving warren of dead-end arroyos. The agents decided to take Castillo along, as a guarantee they would find their way out of these blind canyons that bordered the San Pedro Martir Mountains.

In truth, Enrique had only a vague idea about where the cartel might have a hideout. He was stalling for time. When the trio reached a deserted shallow valley that forked into several sandy riverbeds, Castillo told them to stop. "This is the entrance to the Sal Si Puedes Canyon. The cartel uses these multi-pronged ravines as a diversion."

The agents exchanged dubious glances. There was no sign of any activity. No tire tracks from vehicles. No litter or graffiti. The ground looked as if it hadn't been disturbed for ten thousand years. Still, maybe Castillo knew something. The location might yield some clues. Castillo had months of experience in the area so the other agents deferred to him. "Each of us will take one arroyo. Search the dry creek beds for signs of recent intruders. Look for tracks. Look for hidden rock trails up the canyon walls. Look for caves. Be especially careful if you find a spring."

An hour later, the two agents met back at the Suburban. Tromping through the hot, dusty ravines had been futile. They were drenched in sweat but had found nothing except an old camper shell, the remains of a dirt bike motorcycle and discarded beer bottles.

Still, as they reported to Captain Dolan, they had lost something—Castillo.

Dolan was furious. "Find him if you can. Don't let that screw-up wander around in his underwear, peeping into windows. But you can't stay too long. By three this afternoon, you need to check in again with our counterparts in their ops center in San Felipe. They are coordinating a major offensive in that area. It should start soon in those hills."

35
Capture

Today, Wednesday, July sixth, H was going after his prize. If and when Charley 2 flew into his sector and was about two miles offshore, this would be the moment to strike. The entire operation was tricky and could go terribly wrong. Every detail had to work to perfection.

H had been busy making intricate, careful adjustments to his Decoy interceptor and debugging its missile lock-on protocols. Last week he had collected the electronic codes from the experimental missile the air force had fired at his broken-down beat-up Courtesan. Now his revamped Courtesan and the Predator Decoy were tweaked for the ultimate mission—their meetup with Charley 2.

Shortly before noon, the Predator popped up right on schedule, flying west three miles offshore above Playa Refugio. Two high-performance Reaper drones were shepherding Charley 2, positioned two miles above it, pacing at the same speed of the Predator, mimicking its moves. H guessed they probably had the air-to-air missile.

All was ready. H left the cave and sent off his drones to rendezvous with the Predator. His mothership Courtesan swiftly settled into position six feet above Charley 2, dispatching its cluster of Remoras. The Courtesan was rigged with the electronic defense that made it invisible to the Reaper's Skyfire missile protocols. The new Decoy, shaped like a smaller Predator and filled with electronics to attract their lock-on missile codes, flew into position directly above the mothership. It began mimicking Charley 2's electronic signals. Now the mothership, flying immediately below the Decoy, seized control of Charley 2, disabling its location transponder while feeding it new coordinates and flight instructions. The Predator responded, idling its engine, sinking straight down and descending in a steep dive.

This sudden maneuver should have alarmed the air force console jockeys watching from the cameras on the bodyguard Reapers. But the speed of the takeover and the countermeasures confused everybody. The Decoy, directly above the descending Predator, continued along the Charley 2's flight path, reassuring everyone that all was routine.

In Yuma, the Border Protection pilots had lost their visual feeds but were still getting normal flight readouts. In Nevada, the air force pilots watched an aircraft that looked like the Predator flying normally. They were confident it would continue on its heading.

Only the computers realized something was terribly wrong. It took the Reaper's control units two minutes to detect the Decoy substitution, and only then did it automatically lock on the Skyfire codes for the Decoy.

Within that brief interval, the mothership Courtesan had dropped over a mile with its stolen Predator. At five-thousand-feet, it turned Charley 2 toward the dry lake area where H was waiting.

This was thrilling. H's heart rate shot up as he sat in an old 4-wheel-drive Jeep pickup. He hadn't landed a Predator in years, and never one without its nose camera. Still, this deadstick engine-out arrival seemed easy enough.

The Predator with the smaller Courtesan flying above it turned toward the lakebed to begin the landing approach. H took over with a handheld controller. The drones were coming in hot. He signaled the Courtesan to break away and it did, but there was nothing he could do now for Charley 2. He had to bring it in—there was no chance to go around.

The kidnapped drone's approach speed was thirty miles per hour too fast. H dropped the gear and flared the landing. Charley 2 streaked across the dry lakebed, kicking up a huge dust cloud before skidding to the right and collapsing to its belly. There was no fire but the landing gear was mangled.

The Courtesan landed itself softly. H pulled it into the cave-like hiding place where he stored it and slid a camouflaged shrubbery door closed.

The Predator's crash landing was a major setback, but one he had prepared for. He frantically drove the Jeep to the wreckage, quickly extracted the Predator's batteries and front avionics tray, and then smashed its location transponder and its emergency locator signal. Next, he dragged a sled of ocotillo branches up beside the slightly mangled Charley 2. With the Jeep's front-end winch, he pulled the nearly one-ton wreckage onto the sled before towing it to a natural cave under nearby rocks. There, he used the Jeep to shove the damaged drone off the sled and into the cave's mouth. Working very fast, he camouflaged both openings with debris and ocotillo bushes.

To cover scars from the pileup, he towed the sled back out to the crash-landing site and frantically hauled it over the grooves in the dry lake made by the drone's inverted V tailfins. After a few anxious minutes, the obvious signs of the rough landing were no longer visible from the air.

He had just pulled the Jeep under the rocky outcrop by the dry lake edge when he saw the silver glint of another drone crossing over the site. *Yes, they are looking for Charley 2,* he thought. *And they aren't going to find it.*

H snuck back to the cavern where he had stowed the drone. He emptied its gas tanks. What a beauty. He walked around Charley 2 several times, reverently running his hand over the smooth lines of the Predator's nosecone. This was simplicity and purity of flight. No human pilot to muck it up.

This was his Predator. Screw the government if they ever thought he could give it back. That serves them right for firing him for another's mistake. He would go back and resume his other identity and celebrate. This Predator proved, and he knew it, that he was smarter than all of them.

At this moment, he had only two more wishes—he

wanted to bag Charley 1 next, and he wanted to be left alone.

—∭—

Tank Dolan was not going to leave anyone alone. He stormed through the corridors, cursing and kicking wastebaskets. Hooper was in the break room, finishing off a soda.

"Hooper. My office. Now." The enraged Dolan continued down the hall, looking for the others who had been in the control trailers.

Dolan could barely breathe. Today's debacle was shaping up to be a career low point. He imagined the hours he'd spend at a sink if he was busted to dishwasher. He could even be forced to retire.

Hooper sheepishly entered. Two of his colleagues were sitting on a hard leather sofa, facing Dolan. No one spoke.

The Captain had his eyes closed. He threw a stack of manila file folders at the wall.

"Tell me how it happened?" Dolan was furious.

"I was flying Charley 2 south, down by Playa Refugio, in that op coordinated with the Mexican army. We were to scan isolated canyons in sector 17 northwest of Puertecitos."

"I was on my third westbound run, approximately two miles offshore, when there was the first bump on the monitor, then a second one and finally a third. All telemetry from Charley 2 faltered for a moment but then resumed but we didn't have the recon or nose cameras."

Dolan only nodded.

"For another two minutes, Charley 2 sent out normal telemetry, but then we simply lost all contact. That was it."

Dolan could hardly speak. "What do you mean? That was it."

"Well, sir, by then the real Charley 2 had disappeared. I was apparently flying a lookalike decoy for the last two minutes."

Dolan smashed his fist against the trailer wall. He turned to a second agent. She had been in contact with the liaison officer in Nevada.

"And, agent Tharp, what did the air force Reaper pilots see? Why didn't they see their target drone disappear?"

"Well, sir, they told me there were anomalies in the telemetry but that they had a positive visual contact with Charley 2. It looked like Charley 2. They were confident they still had Charley 2 until their computers told them they were following a decoy. So, they shot down the decoy. The Skyfires worked very…"

Dolan interrupted. "I don't care how well they worked. They shot down a decoy. Who gives a shit about a decoy? Anyone here happy we shot down a decoy?"

Then Dolan posed a question to everyone. "Did any of our crack pilots actually see Charley 2 fly away? I mean…see it?"

"Apparently not. No. Sir, the decoy was in the way."

The third agent spoke up. "The Reapers began a search for Charley 2. Oddly enough, there was no transponder signal from the real Charley 2. They flew a crosshatch grid over the area for four hours. But the Reapers found nothing. No trace. No heat source. No reflective metal. No emergency locator beacon. No sign of a crash." The third agent continued. "It's as if Charley 2 just disappeared from the world."

Dolan was in a rage. "Charley 2 didn't just disappear. It crashed and it's down there somewhere. It may be in shallow water or, if it is on land, the cartel is eating lunch on our drone. They hate those drones. Well, those bastards will get what they deserve in the next couple of days. Our Mexican counterparts know the perps operate out of caves somewhere west of the Playa Refugio area. We are coordinating a major operation against the Equipo 30 drug cartel with the Mexican anti-drug squads and the Mexican army. It will begin soon, possibly tonight or in the morning. Our agents, including you three, will leave here by chopper within two hours to assist the federales. We will swarm the area to find any trace of Charley 2's crash. You should know, too, that our Reapers are now carrying Hellfire missiles. If we find the command post, the Mexicans have okayed using the Hellfire." Dolan paused. "But only if we consult them first."

"Your field work will involve canyon by canyon searching. There's got to be some sign of a crash. Don't forget to bring your snakebite kits and survival gear. In the meantime, we'll keep Charley 1 on the ground. The Air Force Reapers will continue to recon the area, assisting the Mexican federal troops."

"There's a lot of real estate to cover but we'll start and take it quadrant by quadrant. You three will be in San Felipe by sundown. Questions?"

"What about Castillo?"

"What about Castillo?" said Dolan.

"Yeah, Castillo. What do we do with the whacker if we find him?"

"Just bring him back"

"But he disappeared in the canyons today. He sounds like he has a screw loose."

"Just bring him back to the safe house in San Felipe. We need to de-brief him before we bring him back here."

"I'm glad I'm not the agent who is going to de-brief him," laughed Hooper, who mimicked pulling down his shorts.

"Very funny, Hooper."

Another agent added. "Should we tie him up? Maybe he'd like that."

"Just bring him back. He'll be fine."

Dolan wanted to strangle someone. "Agents, this is no fucking laughing matter. Enough bullshit about your fellow agent Enrique Castillo. He knows those hills and the canyons back there. We can use his knowledge. We want anyone who contacts him to inform him of what's going on and get him back to San Felipe. His sat phone has been intermittent. I'm concerned that he lacks up-to-date information, and might undertake some action on his own initiative that will compromise our investigation."

Dolan went back to his office and buried his face in his hands.

It's too bad that little fuck-up Castillo isn't here. I would love to blame the missing Predator on him, he thought. *And I still might. Now I've got to look for a drone and find Castillo too. This is really fucked up. What more could go wrong?*

Dolan would find out soon enough.

36
Thursday

Merc spent the morning in San Felipe, slogging down margaritas with friends on the terrace at the Bar Miramar. He had come north to buy parts to fix the rotting ignition wires in his old pickup. It was the last slim hope that he had to salvage the broken down Chevy truck. On the way home, driving Shay's borrowed Oldsmobile, he pounded on the steering wheel and sang *Run Like Hell* along with the old English group Pink Floyd. *"And the hammers batter down the door, you'd better run."*

He was still slightly buzzed when he pulled up in Punta Gringa. Doc, Shay and Ruby were standing in front of RJ's trailer. They were grim.

Shay rushed up and gave him a hug. "Merc. Kiddo. It was terrible."

"What was?"

"Took him an hour ago. They snatched RJ. Bounty hunters in two pickups. Said he had jumped bail for stealing a bunch of church money in Southern California."

"They took him?"

"They did. In cuffs," said Ruby.

"Did they say what's going to happen?"

Ruby was matter of fact. "Apparently, he had been on trial for embezzling a quarter million church dollars. He blew off the bond and split, hiding out here. Now, he's going back to jail. Possibly for years."

"What about all of his stuff?"

"They only let him take some clothes," said Doc. "RJ said we should split up what we wanted and then give the rest to any poor family we know." Doc tossed him a set of keys. "He said to give you these. They're for his F-150. He said it was much more reliable than that dying crapola Chevy you drive."

Merc took the keys and sat down in RJ's favorite bible reading chair on his porch.

"I can't believe it. How did they find him?"

"His picture," said Doc. "From some Internet posting about my resurrection. Apparently, RJ was standing in the background of a photo. Someone in Southern California recognized him."

"Even with the long hair and beard?"

"Yeah, and that guy Nick was a bounty hunter. He's been looking for RJ," said Doc. "Guess he found him."

"I suspected that about Nick. He was such a sleaze. RJ should have hit the road when this guy first showed up."

"Maybe RJ wanted to be caught. Maybe he was tired of running," said Shay.

"No. There's always another isolated spot to hide. I

really liked RJ. What a pleasant if somewhat strange guy."

The four of them sat for minutes without speaking.

Doc went on. "Another thing. Merc, The ejido came out this afternoon and scraped up the remains of Taras Blubber's burned out house. Put everything in a truck and took it away. All that's left is beach. They said they plan to level every place on the spit by next Monday."

"Son of a bitch. They are moving faster than I thought they would," said Merc.

"Merc. That settled it for me. I've already told Shay and Ruby. I can't take this bullshit anymore. I'm bagging Punta Gringa and heading back to meet Rose and then going off to Idaho for a while."

"When?"

"Probably tomorrow. I'm taking only the important stuff. I'll get as much in the truck as I can. There's not a lot left. They can crush the old shack if they want."

"Yeah, I figured you'd be hooking up with Rose again. It would be nice to have somebody waiting for me." He paused. "I'm going to hit the road but I don't have anyone to go to."

Shay smiled. "Oh, I think a recent dancing partner might be a possibility."

"No. I was tempted but I just don't know."

"You might rethink that. From what I see, someone made you the offer of a lifetime," said Shay. "And I think she is a keeper."

"Merc. I agree, but if that relationship stuff still scares you, and you decide to run away from it, get in touch and come north to stay with me and Rose. Right now, here in Gringa, I've got some extra stuff. Like RJ said, if there's anything you might want, take it. Tools. Furniture. I want to carry as little as possible across that border," said Doc.

Merc thought for a moment. "Not to be an opportunist. But, well, let me ask? Would you loan me your rifle and pistola?"

Doc thought a moment. "That's a tough one. I know you guarded those for me while I was dead. But I love those pieces." Doc paused for a moment. "Listen. Okay. If you'll get them back to me sometime. I don't want to try and smuggle them through the military checkpoint anyhow." Then Doc shifted his feet. "Now, I'll tell you something that will surprise you."

"Oh God," said Merc. "Is this anything I want to hear?"

Doc looked around to see if anyone besides Shay and Ruby were nearby. Satisfied, he went on. "You'll never guess what I've found?"

Merc frowned.

"And maybe you don't want to know," said Doc.

"Go on."

"I heard from a Border Protection agent in town that they are searching for another missing drug enforcement drone, one that had been flying over this area. Somebody shot that one down yesterday."

"The cartel?"

"The agent seems to think they did it."

"And what else?"

"The border agents think someone from around here might be helping them."

"Uh oh," said Merc.

"I would be the prime suspect, but I know it's not

me," said Doc. "So that leaves you, or Ruby, Shay or Eliot."

"Eliot is the only one who might fit the bill, except for some Mexicans in Playa Refugio," said Merc. "But Eliot is such an apolitical recluse. He doesn't seem to do anything but collect weird stuff. I mean, he's probably got some tech smarts but why would he be involved? How could be help them? Doesn't make sense."

"I agree. But I went over to ask him and he wasn't there. He's been quietly cleaning out his house. All his personal stuff is gone. The place is nearly empty except for cattle skulls, bones and mining junk."

"Well. He's probably moved stuff because they're kicking us out. Where do you think he is?"

"He went off to the foothills."

Shay had listened intently without saying a word. She walked over and sat in Merc's lap and put her arms around his neck. She was shaking. "Think about it," she said. "We all need to find somewhere else to live."

Enrique had a troubled Thursday night after he ditched his fellow agents in Sal Si Puedes Canyon. He tried to grab some sleep in an abandoned mine tunnel. Frantic bats made squeaky, clicking noises as they swarmed about in the darkness, keeping him awake. Also, the energy bars were getting tiresome and now he craved real food. It was time to reach into the past to tap some resources.

In the afternoon, he made his way to the highway and then hitched a ride to the Playa Refugio turnoff. From there, he headed back into the foothills to the remote ranchito of Fernando Leon, a longtime family friend and a retired Mexican federal police agent who had worked with his dad. The Castillo children always thought of Fernando as their uncle. The old man was out by his gate.

"Buenas tardes—good afternoon—Tio Fernando."

"Enrique. It is so good to see you." They exchanged enthusiastic abrazos. "Would you like a cup of coffee?"

"I would love that."

Fernando went to a worn cast-iron burner behind the house and poured murky coffee from a percolator. The brown liquid was so acidic that Enrique could feel pain behind his ears. However, this was a man his father always admired and had his sons call uncle. So he was gracious and drank it.

"What brings you to Playa Refugio? Vacation?"

"No. A secret assignment that I cannot tell you about. And I got banged up. I've got a bum ankle and cactus spines in my right hand from chasing bad guys."

"Ah, I've got some of La Gringa's salve for the cactus." Fernando paused. "It's a tough business. I'm worried about you. I heard from one of my old colleagues that you were caught peeking at a woman taking a bath. That's disgraceful. You shouldn't do that."

"I agree, Tio. It was a big mistake."

"Yes, and I heard that La Gringa taught you a lesson."

"Yes, she did. With red ants."

The old man smiled. "I bet you are here as part of the army force that's going to smoke out the cartel in the next two days. I heard it from someone who is still working. He warned me to stay out of the hills from tonight until Saturday. I wish I were up there in the action. I'm bored."

Enrique was surprised about the military offensive. He knew nothing about any upcoming assault. Was he out of the loop by accident or on purpose? Still, this would be a convenient cover story with Fernando. "Si. Yes. Working with them. But don't tell anyone." He drank another sip of the terrible coffee. "Dear Uncle Fernando, my ankle needs to recover. I need to stay here a few days here before I head up into the mountains. Then, perhaps, you could give me a ride west into the foothills."

The old man's enthusiasm was scary. "Into the fire of action. The two of us together."

"No, when the really ferocious army action is over, I'll need to head back toward Sal Si Puedes Canyon. From there, I'll have to go alone. It'll be easier to move through the hills solo when I'm on the trail of cartel bad guys. You understand."

"Okay, but I can't give you a ride—my truck has broken down. You could take one of my nephew's two rusty motorcycles. No one has ridden either of them in years. You can borrow one if you want."

Enrique went back to the shed and inspected the two ancient Honda 90 mopeds with their tiny wheels and miniscule engines. Spider webs and dust covered both. These were the opposite of imposing—they looked downright silly. If Enrique were to ride it, the underpowered machine could barely go thirty miles an hour on pavement. On sand, and in the dirt, it might get him far enough up the road, but it was extremely loud. Still, it was transportation. He'd have to make do.

Fernando walked into the shed. "There's something else I didn't tell you. I heard one of those drones was shot down yesterday near here. Agents are out looking for the crash site."

"How did you hear that?"

"My old friends."

"It's the cartel that probably did it. You know, Tio, that I fly those drones. They've been after mine for a month." He went on in detail about the beauty of the drones, and how he felt like a real pilot when he was at the console. Enrique described the recent skirmishes and explained how the smaller attacking drones would swarm the larger Border Protection craft by coming at them from above.

"Just like the hawks do sometimes," said Fernando.

"Yes, Tio, but hawks strike suddenly."

"Not always. Yesterday when I was watching them soar over the hills, I saw two hawks, one big one below and a little one above it, fly down through these canyons. They stayed together perfectly. It was like one was taking care of the other."

"You sure they were hawks?"

"Well, what else could they be? I thought they were. But my eyesight is very bad."

"Where did they go?

"Inland. Toward the hills."

"And they were flying together?"

"That's what I saw."

"As if it was a mother watching over its child."

"Si."

A grin spread across Enrique's face. The light had gone on. "Of course. That's it. This could be the answer. That's why all this is happening. Why didn't we think of that before?" He hugged his uncle. "Tio Fernando, you have given me a very important clue. Where's your phone?"

"In the casita."

Enrique reached into his backpack and pulled out a notebook with coded cell phone numbers. To bounce his new theory off someone he respected, he punched in a U.S. number.

"Ellen Byrne."

"It's agent Castillo. Border Protection."

"Ah, the missing agent. Did you hear about Charley 2?"

"Just now. I found out it was taken."

"Not taken. The cartel flew a clever decoy up to our Predator and shot down Charley 2. It was offshore and dove straight down from 10-thousand and crashed. Must have gone straight in and hit the water."

"No. No. No. I don't think that is what happened."

"Castillo. It's gone. That's what we can see from the Reaper video. It's the only thing that could have happened."

"No. That's why I'm calling. Listen to me. I've got a theory. Charley 2 didn't crash. They spoofed our drone. They've got him in these mountains."

"Castillo. This is crazy. Still think it's aliens?"

"No. Not aliens. Very real people. I talked to an eyewitness who saw it being guided down. I think we're going to find Charley 2 intact."

"What the hell are you talking about?"

"Listen. Hear me out. First of all. Let's forget the cartel. Why? They hate the drones. It just never made sense that they would keep swarming it, banging on it and not just blow it out of the sky. So I don't think it was the cartel. No, the attacker after our drone wasn't destructive, but in fact was very careful to treat the drone gently. Still, they kept screwing around, bumping Charley 2. I think they were practicing spoofing it. Don't you see? They eventually wanted to bring it down intact. They wanted a Predator. It's got to be someone who needs a drone."

"What kind of a person would want an older model drone?"

"Possibly to sell it on the black market? But it is old technology so that doesn't make much sense. But what if, and this is my theory, what if someone is pissed off at the U.S. government? How about any ex-drone pilot? Why aren't we looking for an ex-drone pilot? Not the cartel. Our perp has gotta be someone who has flown drones before. And someone who knows the guidance electronics. Someone, perhaps, who has worked for a drone manufacturer, writing code or something. That person could easily concoct a scheme to steal it. That person is our magician. He made us look for answers somewhere else."

Ellen Byrne was silent for ten seconds. "You know, that makes sense. Let's see if you are right. I'll get air force to cross check ex-drone pilots with anyone who was worked for three or four of the big companies."

"And then cross-check that with the Mexicans for residents down here with long term immigration cards. Then tell Dolan."

"Where are you? How do I get in touch with you?"

"I might not be at this phone again. I'll call you back tomorrow. And when the army stops the gun battles in the hills, I will go back in. I'm pretty sure I can find the missing Charley 2."

"Okay. Thanks Castillo. Sorry I thought you were a little nutty. I'll buy you a beer when this is over. Right now, I'm on it."

Enrique handed the phone back to Fernando.

"Tio Fernando. I'm tired. Where can I sleep?"

"In the hammock in the back."

"One more thing, Tio. Is it possible for you to ask around and find out when the army thinks it will be finished wiping up the cartel?"

"Claro. I can do that. Now you settle in. I'll go into town."

Enrique was bone-tired but his mind was on fire. All he needed to do was find an ex-drone pilot down here? Find out if that person was in the grip of the cartel bosses. He wondered if the military was going to succeed in rounding up the cartel. Up to now, he hadn't crossed paths with the bad guys, only getting into scrapes with the local residents. But now he was going into the cartel territory. Still, he didn't fear what was next. *I guess,* he thought, *it is going to get exciting.* He lay quietly in the hammock before dropping off to weird dreams and troubled sleep.

Fernando Leon walked into Playa Refugio and bought a gallon of gas, two quarts of oil and picked up four store made bean burritos and a case of bottled water. He also dropped in to visit with his old colleagues at the Mexican military command post.

Back at his tiny ranchito, he woke up Enrique. "The army will be through in two days. You can leave then."

37

The Fire Pit

Chuchu Acosta was standing in Merc's driveway. "I'll give you fifty dollars, a pair of binoculars and a new leather recliner for it."

"Chuchu. We've been friends for a long time. This is a hard-working truck."

"Merc. It's barely working. It's junk. That's my offer."

Even with the new ignition wires, the old Chevy pickup still wheezed, rattled and sputtered. Merc knew it would take a major effort to restore the faltering engine.

"Look. They are going to tear down my shack. I can't use the recliner. How about the money, binoculars, and some gas."

Chuchu thought about it. "Okay, the binoculars, ten gallons of gas and fifty dollars."

Merc agreed. He signed over the Chevy to Chuchu and followed him back into Refugio in RJ's F-150 to pick up his loot. Back in Gringa, he pulled up at Shay's place. She and Ruby were loading boxes into the Oldsmobile.

Ruby gave him a powerful hug. "Merc." She was emotional. Her ever-present reassuring smile was gone, replaced with a worried look. "Merc. I am so frigging sad. Things are going to hell around here. RJ gets dragged away. Doc is leaving. We all have to be out by Monday."

"Yeah. All good things are ending, my dear. The sand-spit is kaput."

"Well, we're leaving Mexico. Shay and I are going to make a trip to a storage warehouse place in Yuma tomorrow morning and then come back for one more load."

"What will you do with all the macramé?"

"I guess I'll leave it at Juanita's in San Felipe. She'll try to sell it."

"I knew you guys would go next. I don't know what took you so long." Spontaneously, he walked up and hugged Shay. Shay was startled. This was totally out of character. Merc never initiated hugs for anyone.

Merc unloaded groceries from his pickup. "Shay. You guys need any help, let me know."

"I think we're all right. Do you want any of our left-over stuff?"

"Do you still have that pistol?"

"Hey, kiddo. Still do. Still have Doc's .45. Never gave it back. Why?"

"Will you loan it to me?"

"No, I'd rather keep it. Might need it. I thought you had a few of Doc's guns."

"I do. He gave me the rifle and the pistol. But there are some things going on here I just don't understand. I'm getting a shitload of subtle and not so subtle warnings. I'd just wanted to be ready if anything happened before I could get out."

"Well, you've got some firepower. I'm finished packing. Ruby has too. After our trip to the border, we'll stay at La Gringa's ranch for a few days before we finally head north for good."

They all sat quietly for a minute. Then Shay spoke. "Merc. You should come up to the ranch. Ever visit the curandera La Gringa?"

"No. I know where her place is, but I don't believe in those voodoo things. Mystics and all."

"You've got to have the right attitude. Yesterday, Ruby and I went to see if she had any answers. We did a session."

Ruby spoke up. "Yeah. I'm not sure I'd go back but it was one helluva experience."

Merc laughed. "That strange? So, what's she like? Did La Gringa read your palms or something? Could she see the future with those scary eyes?"

Shay faced him. "Yeah, those grey eyes are something. But no, Merc, nothing like that. We had a long session. Four bizarre hours. Did chanting and stuff. We drank this awful tea. And then glasses of powerful mescal. She burned incense and we smoked joints. We had to wear tiaras of twigs and necklaces of colored glass with pelican bones, bullets and little plastic manta rays. There must have been a hundred candles. This went on and on."

"I told her about a dream I had, where I was climbing over rocks. Everyone Gringan was there. Everyone had guns. Ruby was also in the dream. You were in this dream too."

Merc stared at Shay. "And what happened then?"

"La Gringa said that these dreams were visions, that they were telling us to be ready. All of us. She said that included her. By then I was pretty far gone on the weed and the mescal. After that she sang unintelligible songs and then, I just don't remember what happened next. I know Ruby dropped into a trance twice, babbling incoherently. The next thing we knew, both of us woke up with bad headaches, throwing up in a field down the road from the sandspit. We were still wearing the necklaces."

"Holy shit," said Merc.

"Holy shit is right," said Ruby.

Shay smiled. "Stay for dinner with us. I've got to clean out the fridge. There's the last of the pasta and marinara sauce in a jar. And, I've got my final two bottles of red wine to drink up."

Ruby stood up. "I'd love to stay for a last supper but I have to take the last of the macramé to the Acostas in Refugio. I told them that I'd stop for a meal there. But I'll see you guys in the morning." Ruby walked out to her truck.

"Yeah, okay. Merc, will you stay?"

"Sure"

"Wanna know something?" said Shay.

"Okay."

"I'm going to miss this place, but it's just too crazy here. RJ hauled off to jail. Doc leaving. The mysterious Eliot business with the drones. The ejido's front loaders scraping away everything out here. I'm thinking eventually I'll end up in Flagstaff. I have friends there. Will you come there and stay with me until this all settles down."

"I'll think about that. I'm packed to go. I'll let Ismael use the *Outta Here.*"

"You aren't getting any younger, kiddo. You might want to have some sort of plan."

"Nah. Hard to plan for the unexpected. I never thought they'd kick us out of here. I thought I'd be here forever."

"Merc. You are the definition of a fatalist. Do you really want to wait for things to happen to you all the time?"

"That's not fair."

"Oh, yes, kiddo. You're a billiard ball. Another one hits you and you just angle off somewhere else."

"Well, why not?"

"Merc, you drive me crazy. You don't believe in anything. You really only want to party and fish."

"Sounds like me."

Shay rolled a joint and they began to smoke it.

"So, what'll we do tonight?"

"Sit back and watch the sky. We've done that sober and we've done that drunk. I fell in love with the stars. They are so magical here and the sky is so black."

Shay grinned. "Yeah, I loved the nights here. There's so little to get in the way."

And that's what they did. After dinner, Shay lit the fire pit on the patio and they sat for hours under the canopy of stars, finishing off the wine and talking about what future destinations would make them happy. In the distance, they could hear muffled gunshots. Trouble was starting back in the hills.

When the fire pit burned down, they went inside and Merc stayed the night. They slept together in each other's arms, not lovers but friends. This was the peaceful finale to the years in the desert.

38

The Takeover

On Friday morning, Merc stuffed four boxes of personal belongings into his Whaler fishing skiff and then trailered the *Outta Here* to Playa Refugio. Ismael from the El Parador was waiting at his home. He would be using the skiff until Merc came back for it.

Ismael was excited by other events. "Merc, it happened. Have you watched any news?"

"What happened?"

"In Mexico City, special squads staged a pre-dawn raid and arrested Bat-Mex owners in the ritzy Coyoacan neighborhood, hauling them off to jail. Federal prosecutors are closing the Bat-Mex company and taking control of everything, including the battery plant in Punta Gringa. I heard the charges were fraud, drugs, dangerous substances, and money laundering."

Ismael continued. "Then they said other Mexican companies were going to absorb Bat-Mex. Energia Frontera in Mexicali will take over the Gringa plant, make it three times bigger, and build an industrial park around it. They even interviewed our own ejido manager Alex in Playa Refugio."

"But no word about the local Bat-Mex guys, such as Francisco. No one has seen him in the last 48 hours. Some tell me he has slipped out of town and is on his way to Guatemala."

"What about the workers?" asked Merc.

"The Energia Frontera people gave the workers the week off. They are going to do a meeting in Refugio tonight to explain their plans for the factory and the site."

"Holy shit," said Merc. "Is it safe for me in town?"

"Sure. Everyone's happy. It looks like there will be more jobs now."

Merc drove two blocks and parked behind El Parador. The street in front of the ejido office was crowded. A noisy group gathered by Acostas convenience store, drinking from the half-gallon cayuamas of beer and arguing loudly about the future. But they quieted down and stared skyward whenever a Mexican Black Hawk helicopter sped across the sky.

The military campaign in the backcountry had intensified. It was common knowledge that the target was the Equipo 30 cartel. Truckloads of soldiers were coming down the road from San Felipe and turning west into the hills. Sporadic automatic gunfire could be heard throughout the day. A few village characters, including the notorious scout Iris Lopez, had fled from Playa Refugio.

At six o'clock Friday night, the Energia officials opened their public meeting in the dirt parking lot next to the delgado's office. Merc stood in the back. Flanked by the ejido officials and the delegado, they explained that the factory would be closed for a week while new supplies were brought in, and then would reopen for processing on Monday. All the workers would retain their jobs. Energia's new manager promised to expand the plant and hire another shift, bringing the workforce up to forty-five.

The news seemed to satisfy the workers. They continued milling around outside the grocery store. As darkness settled in, several brought out guitars and mournful singing began to fill the night air. When the generator blipped off at nine pm and the town went dark, the crowd remained around an impromptu bonfire. They drank, argued, and sang, finally staggering to their homes. As the village quieted, the only sound was the racket of occasional gunfire in the hills to the west.

Before he left town, Merc ran into Alex from the ejido.

"Merc. We have to clean off the sandspit for the new factory. We'll begin with all the empty trailers tomorrow. You'll need to move your stuff to a new mobile home we have for you north of town. Our trucks will help you do that."

"How soon do I need to be out?"

"Well, we've got to make a move quickly. Pack as fast as you can. We'll probably get to your place last. Sometime on Monday."

Merc finally made it back to Punta Gringa before midnight. The battles in the hills continued. Tracer bullets made colorful arcs over his place. Helicopter gunships with searchlights circled to the west. Their constant thudding noise was annoying. He defied logic by sitting out in his patio, poring over maps of possible destinations—hidden retreats along the coasts of Baja. He spent the rest of the time enjoying the night sky.

39

The Battle Spreads

By daybreak on Saturday, the fighting had spread. Three pickups carrying more than a dozen cartel fighters had broken through the siege lines back in the mountains and had stormed the sentry post at the empty battery factory. They barricaded themselves inside. Army units surrounded the perimeter. Snipers inside the plant began shooting at the troops as the helicopters circled overhead.

The chatter of automatic weapons was intermittent but violent. Reinforcements eventually tightened the ring around the plant. They set up a roadblock on the beachfront road to Punta Gringa, cutting off access to the sandspit. Random firefights with those holed up inside continued through the morning.

Shortly before noon, Merc summoned up the nerve to check out the battle. He wandered close to the main gate and watched a few Equipo 30 fighters try to break out, making a run for it by driving a pickup through the wire fence around the side. They headed up a dirt road, disappearing into the foothills. A Black Hawk helicopter followed the car and fired its M60 cannons.

The Mexican commanders launched an immediate frontal attack on the plant, firing rocket propelled concussion grenades and tear gas into the building. The battery factory's wooden roof caught fire and began to burn. The intense heat drove the narco gang members out one by one with their hands up. The soldiers put a hood over their heads and then shoved them into the back of military transport trucks. The suspects were bound for special cells in Mexicali.

In the early afternoon, Eliot came to say goodbye. He had already emptied his house of anything he wanted. "Merc, where's everybody?"

"Doc's gone. Shay and Ruby are packed up and off to La Gringa's. You and I are the stalwarts."

"So, the good times on the sandspit are no more."

"That's it." Merc was bit cool to him. "Doc said that the agents think someone on the sandspit had been helping the cartel. Was that you? Did you put us in danger? How could you have done that?"

Eliot just shrugged. "You weren't in danger from me. I never had anything to do with the cartel. I did have a beef with the U.S. government. There is more to it but I don't have time to tell you. Right now, I have to get back. But you've been a good friend, Merc. I hope we meet up again."

"It's true." He shook Eliot's hand. "And I still owe you."

"No. What happened that day was simply what anyone would have done." And Eliot turned, hopped into his pickup and drove off.

The factory continued to burn, sending clouds of smoke over the sandspit. About nine, with the last daylight fading, rapid gunfire in the hills signaled another fierce shootout had begun. This lasted for an hour then all went quiet. Merc got out his last deck of cards and played solitaire on the patio.

40

A Suspect At Last

Sunday morning, the battle had quieted. Ashes and embers from the burning factory covered the nearby desert and the sandspit community. An army officer came by and told Merc that they had arrested 15 suspects, that four members of Equipo 30 cartel were killed and a few got away during the chaos around the fire. They believed the Cuban was still out in the desert.

Mexican officials were concerned about the pollution. Environmental specialists from PROFEPA donned protective hazmat suits and spread out on the sandspit to take samples. They spent the day clipping bushes, rubbing dust from the old trailers and filling vials with samples from the sandy road. That afternoon, ejido officials declared Punta Gringa a health hazard and ordered everyone to leave as soon as possible.

—⚒—

Sunday afternoon, Tio Fernando returned to the ranchito from San Felipe with news that the military had scored a victory over the cartel and that the dangerous fighting had ended. Enrique asked to borrow the phone.

"Dolan."

"Captain. It's agent Castillo."

"Finally. Do you know what's been going on?"

"Everything."

"That scientist Ellen Byrne told us about your theory. We crosschecked drone pilots who left the service with those who worked with defense and drone manufacturers. There were about a hundred names."

Enrique groaned.

"But we checked that against persons with long-term Mexican immigration papers and we have a match. Someone named Steve H. Jantzen. He left the agency after a misguided drone strike in Afghanistan. My sources say he got a raw deal. But then, as a civilian, he worked for FlyTomics. Now his address in Mexico is San Felipe."

"Jantzen. I haven't run across anyone by that name, but I'll keep it in mind."

"So, will you come back to San Felipe and help us find Charley 2?"

"That's where I'm headed now, Captain."

"San Felipe?"

"Yes, I'll get there. But after I check out the report of two aircraft flying together in the foothills. And I'm still looking for the fiberglass guy from Punta Gringa. He might know the Cuban. After that, I'll come right to San Felipe."

"Good."

So at 4:30 in the afternoon, a rested, well-fed border agent mounted a skinny rusted Honda moped scooter and set out from his uncle's ranchito west of the highway. He had a backpack full of food and was headed for Sal Si Puedes Canyon, the formidable area where he ditched his fellow agents.

At last the picture was clearer. It made sense. Now Enrique even had had a name of a suspect he could hunt—Steve Jantzen.

And he had a location. While he was exploring one of the sandy arroyos after he ditched the two San Felipe border agents last week, he had come upon fresh foot-prints along an older abandoned trail. From his days as a field agent, he knew that any activity in these canyons was highly unusual. If he began there, maybe the trail would lead to a spot where it left the sand and ascended into the rocky hillside.

41

Could Have Had
Him Any Day

"I'm not coming out. You'll have to fucking drag me out."

Merc yelled through his window at the ejido officials and Padre Nacho. They were standing in front of a bulldozer and a large semi that would hall away the debris.

His final day on the sandspit was exactly four years from the morning he arrived. At that time, Punta Gringa was a dysfunctional mellow community of 40 lost souls, all hiding out in their own particular way.

Now Merc was the last of the ratas. There was no chance Punta Gringa would ever relight and he knew it. In a fit of margarita-fueled pique and misguided sentimentality, he called the new ejido managers and told them he was going back on his promise to leave gracefully. He ranted about the new condos and vowed to barricade himself.

That afternoon, Merc's house and his old Streamlite on blocks were the only objects in the path of an empty sandspit. Ejido workers had flattened Doc's empty house, towed away Ruby and Shay's old trailers, and had demolished Eliot's cabin after hauling off his collection of skulls and bones to the dump.

With Merc looking on from inside the one room shelter he built, the tractor-like front loader hooked up a beefy chain to the Streamlite trailer and dragged it off its blocks, towing it to the roadside, crushing it and lifting the wreckage to a waiting truck.

Padre Nacho was on his side. "Merc, Gaby called me and that's why I'm here. It's over. You've got to come out. If you do, you will be in my custody. If you don't leave voluntarily, they'll come in and arrest you. Then, you might be immediately deported. We both know they can force the issue."

Merc yelled back. "I'm not coming. The ejido broke its promises that we could stay on this land. They probably won't use it for a parking lot. I'm sure it's going to be rich folks condos. Their word obviously isn't worth a shit. I can't believe any deal they offer."

"Merc, they are going to demolish your house today. I don't want them to do that with you in it. I like you Merc. You have a good heart."

"I like you too, Padre. You have a better heart. But you can tell them to go screw themselves." Merc yelled through the window. "I'm staying."

There was a heated discussion with Alex. Finally, the Padre picked up the bullhorn again. "Merc, get out. This land is damaged. Polluted. It will never be good for living again. There are thousands of miles of desert shoreline available to you. You could go south to Gonzaga Bay or Bahia de Los Angeles, or over to the Pacific coast, or to

Descanso, where there may be welcoming arms. Wherever you go, I have many connections. I'll guarantee that you'll be able to find a beautiful place."

"No way. I love this space. If the rich get their hands on it, then no one will be able to enjoy it." He was standing by the window, staring out at the officials.

The Padre put down the bullhorn and walked toward the house. Merc stepped out onto the front porch to talk. No one could hear what was said. Merc shrugged and appeared to nod yes and then went back into the house. Padre Nacho turned and said, "He's coming out."

But while Merc had been on the porch, two burly federales snuck in through the back door. Inside, they took him down, throwing him to the floor. He was manacled, dragged out in front of the house and laid face down in the sand.

The Padre was incensed. "No, No. Why are you doing this? He agreed to leave." He demanded that they take the handcuffs off him.

Alex from the ejido walked over and knelt down beside Merc. "I am telling you this, Merc, you should be arrested for the stupidity of defying me. I am the president of the ejido. However, we have made a deal with Gaby and this is what is going to happen. We will take your furniture to the ejido shed in town. You can collect it there. Gaby arranged for a temporary casita north of town. We will put your personal stuff in Padre Nacho's pickup. He will give you a ride."

"Then tell me it's for the factory. If that's what is going to happen, I'd feel better about it. But don't lie. I know you are selling it for condos."

"What the hell do you care what we do with it. It's

our land, not yours, foreigner. You've been getting a cheap rent from the ejido for years. Now we can make it pay."

"So, the condos for the rich folks story is true. Goddam," said Merc.

The workers wrestled Merc into the Padre's pickup. Two squads from the ejido moved in and salvaged the stove and refrigerator, the non-working solar panels from the roof, and the windows and doors. The front loader roared to life and with one powerful charge, crashed into the side of the house, knocking it over. It continued crushing the lumber until it could easily lift the rubble in a giant scoop and drop it into the empty trailer.

Finally, not a stick remained. They had scraped off the last footprint of the ratas. Everything was gone. The beach had a messy, rumpled look, but it was level. And polluted. Now the surveyors could get to work. Nothing was blocking the way of progress.

The Padre drove Merc to a small casita north of town. Two agents followed them, with orders not to let Merc out of their sight.

"This place had belonged to Gaby. It's yours for as long as you want it."

"I won't be here long, Padre. Thanks for you help. Would you like a beer?"

"Never refuse one," he said.

Merc unloaded his boxes and opened two beers. Padre Nacho sat beside him as they looked out toward the Sea of Cortez.

"I feel there's more trouble coming," said Merc.

"I can understand that. I've heard much the same. But I have some advice for you."

"Which is."

"Stay tight with the friends you've got. They will bring you through this."

"Yes, that seems to be all that counts now."

The Padre left but Merc remained on the patio. The agents sat in their car on the other side of the casita. The shoreline was just fifty yards away. But this was not the sandspit. Everything about this land was wrong. It seemed like a suburb. Village houses surrounded him. The wind swept harshly through the neighborhood. The tranquility was gone. RJ and Doc were missing. Eliot was off in some bizarre canyon. Ruby and Shay were bunking at La Gringa's ranch. The *ratas* were going their own ways. Merc wondered how he could follow the Padre's wise words.

He had to escape. Merc checked on his minders and then slipped down to the water's edge. He hurried along the beachfront until he was at the seawall by the Refugio Lagoon. From there, he made his way up to Ismael the waiter's house, where he had hidden RJ's old Ford F-150. He threw his personal stuff from the Whaler into the pickup.

The next stop was the 24-hour Pemex station south of San Felipe, where he filled the pickup's tank and three portable five gallon plastic gas cans and bought a case of bottled water. On the way back, with the headlights off, he used moonlight to pick his way along two dark coastal sandy roads, until he could park RJ's old truck a few blocks behind the casita and out of sight from the minders. He snuck the boxes into the tiny house.

Inside, he mixed up a pitcher of margaritas. Merc removed Doc's pistol and rifle that had been wrapped in an ancient sleeping bag. For the next two hours, he finished off several drinks while methodically disassembling and cleaning each weapon. He also reloaded the ammunition magazines. There was nothing more to do. He was armed and slightly drunk. Normally, this was the moment he would hit the road.

Something bothered him. Ever since Francisco Arcangel's last warning, Merc feared that his next step would be to confront a mysterious and unknown enemy. He changed into a black sweatshirt, jeans and boots. He moved the family pictures, his files and everything he cared for back into the pickup's locked toolboxes. Merc rolled up five burritos from whatever food he could find and added those to a half dozen bottles of water in the backpack. Feeling sentimental and fatalistic, he wrote out a note to Padre Nacho about what to do with his things if he didn't come back.

Then he grabbed the guns, the backpack and another jacket. Looking out his window, he could see the minders were still distracted reading newspapers in the stakeout car. Merc left the light on, crept out the back and headed to San Felipe. Gaby had written out directions to her temporary casita. It was time for a long-promised drink with a scorpion.

—w—

In Sal Si Puedes Canyon, Enrique felt lucky. He was carefully following the fresh footprints two miles further up the ravine. Progress was slow. Darkness forced him to camp for the night behind an ocotillo bush in the sandy wash. He closed his eyes sporadically, worried that some-one might get the drop on him.

Early Monday afternoon, tired and aching from the uncomfortable ground, he lunched on a burrito and half a bottle of water before pushing further up the canyon, following the sandy footpath. When the trail left the canyon floor and started to snake up the barren ravine wall, Enrique set out climbing up that trace. It was dangerous. He was out in the open. Finally, he reached two rocky outcrops and he could rest. He settled in to plan his next moves.

Footsteps.

A man with a heavy backpack was picking his way up the narrow path on the canyon wall. Agent Castillo jumped from behind the rock and stuck the Glock in the hiker's face. "Stop. Federal border agent. Don't move."

Eliot had been daydreaming and now was looking down the barrel of an automatic pistol. "What the fuck? Who are you?"

"I am U.S. Customs and Border Protection Agent Enrique Castillo. I'll bet you know the man who does fiberglass repair in Punta Gringa."

"What are you talking about?"

"I was in his house. I saw your picture in his house. In fact, I have it here." Castillo unfolded the picture of the *ratas*.

"You were in whose house? Where?"

"In Punta Gringa. It's got all the cattle skulls."

"Well, yes, that's um…his. But why the pistol?"

"You could be dangerous. I need to know where to find the Cuban?"

"I don't know what you are talking about."

"The Cuban. From the cartel. The fiberglass expert worked on his little plane."

"I don't know any Cuban. I've never met a Cuban."

"The guy with the goatee said the Cuban lived in Puertecitos."

"I didn't know he knew where the Cuban lived," Eliot said.

Castillo now was in a quandary. He hadn't planned on this. He was holding a gun on someone who didn't know anything about it. He had captured an unnecessary prisoner. He guessed he could take him back down to the sandy canyon wash and then tie him to a tree. Or maybe just leave him tied up near the moped.

He used Eliot's belt to bind his hands and sat him on a nearby rock. Then he dug around in the backpack but what Eliot said was true—it contained only food and water. He returned the pack and pulled him up.

"We're going to walk down the rocks and then back through the sand. Don't try anything or I'll use the Glock on you."

Eliot spoke softly. "Easy. Stay calm, homeboy, I'm in a walking mood."

Once back on the canyon floor, they followed the trail and began crossing the dry sandy riverbed. Without warning, they were facing an intruder silhouetted by the afternoon sun. Castillo pulled the Glock and fired but missed. The man yelled.

"Enrique."

Castillo put his gun away. "Tio Fernando. I almost shot you. What the fuck are you doing here?"

"I was bored. I thought you could use some help. So who is your prisoner? From the cartel?"

"No, just someone from Punta Gringa who might know something."

Eliot jumped into the conversation. "I don't know any cartel guys."

"You shut the fuck up," warned Enrique.

"Where are you taking your prisoner?"

"I thought I'd take him back to...to...I don't know. He's not really a prisoner. I thought I tie him to one of the blue palm trees down by my motorcycle."

"Why am I your prisoner? What have I done?"

Castillo pointed the pistol directly at Eliot. "I told you to shut up."

Ex-agent Fernando Leon was beginning to worry about the young Castillo. He seemed overly jumpy. Not composed. Maybe he was under a lot of pressure. This whole scenario didn't make sense. If he was going to chase the bad guys, he didn't need to be watching over a prisoner.

"Enrique. Listen. Why don't we go back to the motorcycles and get them and then we can walk this guy back to the road? You can call for agents to take him to a safe house. Then you and I can go back into the hills and nab the bad guys. Okay."

Castillo thought about it for a minute. "Okay, good idea." He motioned for Eliot to stand up. As he did, he realized that four men had appeared from behind a nearby mesquite bush. They were pointing guns at the three of them.

"What the hell?"

"Don't move, old man. And you too, Castillo. Don't even flinch. Put down your guns."

Fernando Leon, the bored retiree and agent back in action only for two hours, was now a hostage for the first time in his life. This was humiliating.

—∿—

The four with pistols and automatic weapons tied their captives' hands behind their backs. The man with a Cuban accent was the apparent leader. With him were Francisco Arcangel, the former Bat-Mex factory manager, and two tough-looking gunmen.

The Cuban pocketed Castillo's Glock and rigged the straps so Eliot could carry his backpack. The small caravan did an about face and the prisoners marched back up the canyon.

"Move along. When we get to the cave, we have a job we want you to do for us."

Eliot was silent. Castillo wondered what cave the Cuban was talking about. Is it possible this guy might know who stole his Predator?

After they struggled up the path along the steep rocky slope, they entered a narrow passage between two tall rocks that opened up to a flat area in front of the cave. Eliot was untied so he could uncover the mouth. Once the sunlight streamed in, everyone could see the tables were set up with model drones, engines, batteries and communication gear. There were wire leads that connected to satellite dishes set up in rocks above the cave. Flat screen monitors were sitting on workbenches. Rows of batteries were hooked together.

Enrique was fascinated. *So this cave is his ops trailer. Someone must have dragged all the equipment up the rocky trails and built this command center. The prisoner he had captured knew how to get in.* But Castillo was baffled about how this all related to the cartel.

The captives were pushed roughly up against the cave wall and forced to sit. The Cuban came over and squatted down in front of them.

"Eliot Wright. Very cute alias. We know all about you, Jantzen. Steve Honus Jantzen. We know you were CIA and flew drones in Afghanistan and that you worked for the FlyTomics in California where you helped design experimental UAVs. We know you were the pilot who did an airstrike on a village in Afghanistan that killed civilians. We also know that the military blamed you. But we just didn't know how to find you."

Eliot didn't say anything. He looked away.

The Cuban continued. "We were wondering if you could help us shoot us down a drone."

"No, I can't. I'm all out of drones. I used up the last ones last week. I was planning to make more starting today."

For Castillo, this was a culminating moment. He had found this Steve Jantzen. Not only located him, but was tied up next to a genius who had created a drone fleet out of cheap, simple materials. His aircraft had flummoxed all the high priced brainpower of the Customs and Border Protection, the U.S. Air Force and FlyTomics.

The Cuban turned to Fernando. "Old man, what are you doing here?"

"What is your name?" asked Fernando.

"Omar. I am Omar. Why are you here?"

"I cannot say."

Omar slapped the old man's face lightly. "Try again."

"My nephew borrowed my motorbike. I came to find him."

Omar laughed out loud. "That is the stupidest thing you will ever have done. I am not sure what I will do with you now."

"Fuck you," said old Tio Fernando.

The Cuban laughed and turned to Eliot.

"And how long, Mr. Drone Builder, would it take to assemble something that can take down a drone."

"A week."

The Cuban ordered the others to meet at the cave's entrance. Because it was rapidly getting dark, they made plans for the night. Francisco and Omar would take turns outside the cave, one sleeping while the other stood watch. The two gunmen stayed inside as guards.

Eliot and Enrique sat side-by-side propped up against the dirt wall. Enrique was fascinated. He had located his arch-enemy, something no other Border Protection agent had done. Yes, El Agulia was a screw-up, but his methods worked.

Eventually, each captive dozed fitfully. They were tied in a sitting position and it was uncomfortable.

The two guards hung around Eliot's beer cooler in the back of the cave. During the night, Eliot managed to free his hands. He fumbled in his coat's lining and pulled out the cell phone they missed when they searched him. He punched up Merc's number and managed to whisper "Merc, Sal Si Puedes," before the guards caught on. The gunman rushed over, stepped on Eliot's hand and ground the cellphone into the dirt, crushing it against a rock. The other guard kicked Eliot in the stomach. The force of the kick pitched Eliot on his face into the dirt.

The Cuban heard the commotion and came back inside.

"Calling home, Eliot?" He inspected what was left of the phone. "No one can help you now."

Then the Cuban threw the phone back in the dirt. He shot a disdainful look at the guards. "How could you miss that phone? You two are idiots." He pushed the man back against the cave wall.

42

Hellfire

 Eliot slept fitfully and was awake before dawn. His body ached and his stomach was painful to the touch. After the phone incident, the guards would not let him have any water.

The Cuban and Francisco were both outside, arguing loudly. Omar walked back in and strode over to the captives. He squatted down in front of Eliot. "Can you build anything faster than a week?"

Eliot was hurting. He looked up with a grimace and said "No. The fiberglass takes time to dry."

"Then what good is all this equipment?" said Francisco.

"I can watch their drones and see what they are doing."

"Let's do that today," said the Cuban. "Where is the power switch?"

"On the console by the wall. But if you turn on the system, they will know we are here. And I'm sure they would launch a Hellfire missile from the Reapers. No, I wouldn't do that."

Enrique was awake and listening in. He was impressed with Eliot's resistance. If we get out of this, he would be someone good to know. He might love to play video golf.

The Cuban stuck a pistol in Eliot's face. "I'm not so sure you are telling me the truth. If I push the button, maybe something else happens. But if you are right, then you are really no good for us. And after that call last night, then you really are trouble. We should get rid of you."

—⁓—

The pillow smelled of roses; the sheets clean and fresh. Sunlight streamed in the window. Nearby, gulls circled and squawked. He could hear waves crashing. Had to be near the sea. Pulled Gaby closer and lightly planted a kiss below her ear. There was no rebuff this time, only a friendly moan.

Merc's aversion to relationships was in serious jeopardy. He spent the last few years avoiding emotional entanglements. The ratas had been his family.

He hoped this idyll at Gaby's would last for another day. A week.

Coffee. Coffee would be nice. What time is it? He reached over to the side table and picked up his mobile. It was off. When he powered it up, there was a message. It was from Eliot and it was desperate. "Merc. Sal Si Puedes."

Why now? Why Sal Si Puedes? Why the hell now?

There was no other way. He was going to have to leave. She needed an explanation.

"I owe him. We were out fishing one day, very successful, pretty far from shore. Sharks began to show up. When I tried to whack one with a pole, I lost my footing and tumbled off the rail. As I fell, I cut my forehead on a cleat. There I am in the water, bleeding and stunned. Starting to sink. Even with the sharks nearby, Eliot jumps in, pulls me out, stops the bleeding and gets the water out of my lungs. He saved my life. It's now payback time."

Gaby was drowsy. Her voice was raspy. "Hijole. That was very brave."

"Yes it was. So I owe him. I have to go."

"I can understand that," Gaby said. "But can't you wait until it's dark. Shouldn't you wait until tomorrow?"

"No. It's urgent. This sounds dangerous. I'd better go now."

Gaby wrapped her arms around his neck. Her roses overwhelmed him. "Merc, this has been wonderful. I'm leaving tomorrow for Playa Descanso. You must call me there on my mobile. I truly want to see more of you. Perhaps, we are flirting with destiny."

"I will. I promise."

"Then be safe. Vaya con Dios." And she gave him a long, soulful kiss.

Merc drove south from Gaby's San Felipe house. The weather had become humid and the sky was filled with thunderclouds. Sudden torrential rain would make it dangerous in the foothill streambeds west of Playa Refugio. There could be flash floods.

The dirt road heading into Sal Si Puedes Canyon ended after three miles, and from there Merc edged RJ's pickup slowly in tough off-road conditions along the dry sandy wash. It was a crapshoot to pick the right arroyo where they might be holding Eliot. All the canyons looked alike. Wrong choices might mean hours of wasted time.

He drove the old Ford F150 carefully. It only had rear wheel drive. The pickup reached a narrow spot in the dry wash and spun its tires in the loose sand. It was now buried up to its axles. Before abandoning the stranded pickup, he covered it with loose shrubs, then shouldered his backpack, strapped on the assault rife and stuck the semi-automatic pistol his field jacket. He also brought the binoculars.

After another half mile of difficult hiking, he bumped into a clue. It was a Bat-Mex SUV with its wheels buried in the sand. Further along, he found two old Honda 90 motorbikes pushed to the side. Both were leaking fresh oil.

It's like a frigging parking lot up here, he thought. There must be a convention. I am on the right track.

From there, the rocky walls steepened as the trail wound along the canyon bottom. Other than a few boulders and ocotillo bushes, there was little cover to hide his approach. His boots kept crunching loose rocks and making noise.

One mile further, another trail branched off and started climbing the canyon wall. Following that would mean traversing a barren hillside with no cover.

This was an alien place he had never explored. Obvious caves were beginning to appear in the sandstone hillsides. He expected lookouts but it was eerie—there was no sign of any activity. Maybe he was on the wrong trail. Still, he started up the slope.

Scanning the ridges proved fruitless. There was

nobody in sight. Rounding a bend, he began to hear voices from across the canyon further up the arroyo. Using the binoculars, he could see what looked like a cave mouth behind some rocks. Surprisingly, it had a palapa out front.

Merc readied his pistol and the automatic rifle. He carefully climbed down to the canyon floor and crossed the dry river. Then, he slowly worked his way back upslope, moving from boulder to boulder, until he was fifteen meters from the cave opening.

Two men were talking by the entrance to the cave. He recognized the Cuban and his old enemy, the factory manager Francisco Arcangel. Was this everybody? Merc had moved to a position behind a rock, and now was ten meters from the cave opening.

"Omar. Francisco. I have guns trained on you. Put your hands in the air. Don't fucking move or make any sudden gesture. I will kill you very quickly."

The Cuban was calm. "Well, I believe it is Senor Mercury. So you were the one he called. I wondered who would be stupid enough to try and save this pendejo. I didn't expect it would be you." Both men had raised their hands. "Yes, I have your idiot friend Eliot. He's inside."

"Bring Eliot out of the cave."

"You'll have to come and get him."

"No, you bring him out. Otherwise, I will shoot right now." He fired one shot at their feet.

The Cuban agreed. He went into the cave and dragged Eliot out by his bindings. When Merc saw him, Eliot was bent over in the fetal position, and it was obvious he was suffering.

Before Merc could react, two gunmen burst from the

cave, firing machine pistols wildly in Merc's direction. Bullets were ricocheting off boulders everywhere. He was clearly outgunned and trapped in his position behind a rock. He couldn't fire wildly, or he might hit Eliot, who was lying on the ground.

The gunmen with the automatic weapons ran to the sides. Merc could only sit back and lie still, hoping they would make a mistake and he could escape back down the trail. He was still hunched down when one attacker circled around behind him and stuck a gun barrel in his face. "Get up," he gunman demanded. He took Merc's weapons and marched him to the cave mouth.

Once again Merc was standing beside the Cuban. "So, you came on this suicide mission. You are crazier than I thought. I told you we had nothing to do with your friend Doc. That was a little lie. We had grabbed him to teach him a lesson. But we never intended to hurt him. That's why we let him go."

"I don't believe you."

"Why would I lie?"

"Because you're an asshole who works for the cartel."

Francisco Arcangel walked out of the cave and swung a stick, hitting Merc in the side of the face. Stunned, he fell to the dirt.

Francisco kicked him in the side. "Stupid pig," he said. "I've wanted to do this for some time. If it weren't for you and that stupid environmental woman, nobody would ever have noticed and we'd still have the factory. Kill him," he said to Omar.

The Cuban looked up. "No, let's keep him for a couple of hours. He might be valuable."

"One hour. Then I will personally kill him."

Merc was woozy. The blow to the head left a throbbing welt on his scalp. His eyes wouldn't focus.

Francisco Arcangel was clearly in charge. The gunmen dragged Eliot back inside, then wrapped Merc's wrists with duct tape and added him to the captives. He found himself sitting next to an elderly Mexican man, the drug agent Castillo and Eliot. This was rather a pathetic scene.

Eliot was in bad shape. His face was bruised and dirty and he clearly winced at his painful injuries from the beating. Still, he turned to Merc.

"Hey. Thanks for coming," he groaned.

"Hey. Thanks for jumping in that day and swimming with the sharks."

"Sorry. This doesn't look it's going to turn out well."

"An understatement."

"I'd like to say I think they will let you go."

"They aren't going to let me go," said Merc.

"I guess not. Sorry about that."

"Yeah, me too," said Merc.

Enrique was thrilled to be sitting next to Eliot. "Hey, I've been thinking. It's so awesome. You were very clever in how you attacked my drone. We never expected a blind spot approach."

"It was easy enough. Remember, I helped write the code for the Predator. I also had a lot of experience with the air force and the agency. So I knew how you guys would work the problem. So I trained you to fly certain patrols."

"You trained us?"

"Sure. I led you guys around by the nose."

"What the hell was out in the Sea of Cortez? Did you transmit from there?"

"No, those were just decoy transmitters to get you to chase them. While you were doing that, I could keep visual track of you. That way I could lead you to the best intercept spot—two miles offshore."

"Well, you must have been upset when we shot down one of your homebuilt attackers? With the air-to-air missile."

"How about this? You guys didn't shoot it down. I blew up that Courtesan before your missile hit it. By the time I did, I had stolen the missile lock-on codes."

"Courtesan. What's that?" asked Enrique.

"It's what I call the mothership."

"Wow. Man. Your plan was so cool. What did you call the little ones it dispatches?"

"Those are Remoras."

"That is so awesome. You are the bomb, man."

Merc was uncomfortable. He couldn't turn his body and he was sitting on a rock. This shoptalk about the drones bugged him. "Eliot, cut the crap. Where was your mind? This situation is fucked."

"Old grudges, Merc. Besides, it wasn't the drone that got us into this mess. It's the cartel. And from what I understand, these guys are on the run. So, they don't have much to lose. And they don't need a lot of baggage."

One of the guards came over and demanded the pair keep quiet. When Eliot told him to go fuck himself, he kicked Eliot in the stomach one more time. "I can do this all day," the guard said.

Merc sweated uncomfortably. There was no way to get his hands loose. The Cuban returned.

"Okay, boys, this is what we are going to do. We are going to take the old man back to the road and let him go. But the three of you, well, we can't take you with us. Sorry."

Francisco started packing up critical supplies into two backpacks. They gagged Fernando and dragged him outside.

Then they came for Merc. "Eliot," said Francisco, "time is up. We were hoping you could do something for us. But now we don't need you anymore. So we will have to do away with you and your friends. And, unless you can think of a constructive way to help us, Mercury Stiles goes first."

Francisco signaled to the gunmen who grabbed Merc and roughly dragged him along the rocky cave floor.

"Adios," said Merc.

43

The Furies

Merc was being shoved out of the cave. There was very little chance he would get out of this alive.

One of the gunmen seemed edgy. He kept scanning the hillsides. Seconds later, a single rifle shot rang out. It tore through his face and knocked him backwards into the rocks. Then, from both sides of the palapa, more deafening gunfire. Stray bullets ricocheted dangerously around the cave opening. Merc heard some-one scream in Spanish. He watched as Francisco Arcangel doubled over and fell to the ground. The second gunman moved off to the side and began wildly firing with the machine pistol, but there was no sign he connected. The air stunk of gunpowder.

The firefight continued and there was more yelling in English. The second cartel gunman was ripped with bullets and staggered back into the cave and collapsed. Omar also ducked inside, with one bloody hand covering what appeared to be a stomach wound. He picked up the rucksack that Francisco had carried, grabbed a pistol, and ran out to a side trail, disappearing into the hills.

It was over in less than two minutes. The gunfire stopped. Merc was still lying in the cave's opening when he heard new footsteps outside. And familiar voices. In a few seconds, Shay came hopping around the corner, holding her .45 in both hands with her arms extended. She was wild-eyed and wearing a necklace with bones and drones and plastic manta rays. Ruby appeared on the other side, poking her rifle at two fatally injured gunmen and Francisco, and collecting their weapons.

"They're all dead." Ruby reported back. She was also wearing a choker of tiny drones, bones and manta rays. "I can't believe I actually shot someone."

Shay ran over and gave Ruby a hug. "You did fine, Kiddo," she said. Then she walked back and peeled off the tape from Merc's arms and wrists. "How are you doing, Kiddo?" she asked. Ruby touched the vile bruise on his cheek. "You got a pretty good whack there, Amigo."

"What the hell are you guys doing here? How'd you know…?"

"Gaby called us at Athena's. Told us about Eliot's message. Said she thought you were headed up Sal Si Puedes Canyon. So we checked it out on Google, then drove here and found your trail and followed it."

Merc looked around frantically. "The Cuban?"

"He's gone. Run off into the hills."

"We've got to follow him," said Merc, as he stumbled to his feet.

"Don't worry," said Shay. "He's already being followed. He won't get away."

"No, No. We've got to get him. We can't let him escape." Merc struggled, rubbed his eyes, grabbed his pistol and started running after Omar.

The landscape handed an advantage to the escaping Cuban. The path led to a maze of smaller trails across the stark hillside studded with human-sized boulders. The lack of cover made it a perfect spot for an ambush. There were nearby caves—all places to hide. Merc began to follow drops of blood on the rocks. The wounds left a clear trail. But the Cuban was armed, so Merc would stop, listen, and then carefully move ahead.

Within ten minutes, as Merc inched slowly past a massive rock formation, he heard labored breathing. Keeping his finger on the trigger of his semi-automatic pistol, he crept into a clearing to find the Cuban lying on the ground, tied with rope. The air smelled of goats and citrus.

He stuck the pistol against the injured Cuban's head. "Tied up. How in the hell did you get tied up?"

Omar, clearly hurting, looked at him, dazed. "The woman…"

Merc said, "I should kill you. But I won't. I'll let your drug friends in jail take care of you."

He cinched the Cuban's hands with his belt. Grabbing the rucksack and the pistol, he began dragging him back to the cave.

Shay showed up to help. She laughed. "I told you he wouldn't get away."

"How did you know?"

"Can't you smell what's in the air? It's obvious we had help. Athena. This dirtbag had no chance to escape the

Furies. We knew how this would turn out. We all had a vision."

Back inside the cave, Ruby had untied Eliot. Enrique and Fernando remained bound and gagged. Shay taunted Castillo with her pistol. "Let me shoot him in the balls, Merc."

"No, Shay. We can't do that," said Ruby.

"Who is the old man?" asked Shay.

"He's an old friend of Castillo. We can let him go," said Eliot. "Let's untie Castillo, too."

"Why?" said Shay. "That idiot stuck a gun in my face. He would have killed me."

Merc turned toward Castillo. "Our agent will be useful."

The rescuers looked around the cave. "Eliot, what the hell is all this?" said Shay.

Eliot sat down and recounted his year of work to takeover a Predator. He explained how he had left plenty of clues for the government boys to suspect that the cartel was behind this. He smiled broadly when he told them he had brought down a Predator and had it hidden in the hills.

Once again, from a purely tech standpoint, this truly impressed Enrique. *This guy,* he thought, *should be working for us.*

Merc was now confused. He never wanted to be involved with the narco traffickers, and now here he was, part of a shootout that left three members of the cartel dead and a fourth severely injured.

Merc took the gag off of Enrique. He loosened the bindings on his arms.

"Please don't kill me," Enrique pleaded.

"We aren't going to kill you."

Shay pointed her gun again at his groin. "No, I know what we are going to do. Make him a soprano."

Everyone turned toward Eliot. "How about this? What we are going to do is drag the bodies down the canyon to the clearing. Then we fire a lot of guns, leaving around shells as evidence. Fernando will contact the Mexican authorities."

"Then here's the deal with Enrique and Fernando. They forget they ever saw any of us. Enrique also calls his office and tells them of the location of the gunfight and the bodies. He and Fernando meet them there. This gives you, Enrique, credit for wiping out the last of the Equipo 30 cartel."

Enrique smiled. "That's good. I did find them."

"You can tell them you and Fernando shot it out with him."

"That's good."

"And you will never tell them about us...or about me," said Eliot.

"How can I do that?" Enrique asked.

"Figure it out. Just do it."

"What about this cave?" Merc asked.

Eliot outlined his plan. "Easy. Once we get everyone out of here, I will start transmitting. The drones will lock on and should fire a missile. This will set off the pile of explosives I stole from that jerk Taras Burbank's house. I was going to destroy this place, anyhow. That will also tell everyone where we are. So, we'll have to get out fast."

"But I can't return without the missing Predator," Enrique said.

Eliot smiled. "Precisely. This is the best deal. The Predator becomes our get out of jail free card. In 24 hours, when we are all away from here, I will text Enrique and tell him where to find the Predator."

"How do I know you will do that?"

"You don't. But I will do it. Trust the word of a fellow drone pilot. In return, you will never, never tell the true story. As far as you know, you stumbled on these guys in a clearing and surprised them, killing three and taking the Cuban hostage. And, they told you where to find the Predator. Then the missiles blew up the cave."

Castillo thought about the offer. Fernando told him to take it and agreed to corroborate his side of it. "Stories," Fernando said. "You know your father and I did many illegal things. We never told our commanders the truth about the real way these things happened."

Merc interrupted. "Hey guys, hate to stop the chitchat but we have to see if agent Castillo is on board."

Eliot went on. "Think about it, Enrique. Fernando will get part of the credit. And, you, agent Castillo, have saved the day."

Enrique could see the presidential citation on the wall. 'Sounds like it will work. Once more. How can I be sure you will tell me about Charley 2?"

"You can't," said Eliot. "But I said I will do it and I will."

There was a loud bang. A muted buzzer started beeping. Eliot turned to scan the consoles. "Hey. We're in trouble. Big trouble."

Merc turned to him. "What?"

"It looks like one of the cartel tweaks already had

turned on the transmitter. It's been hot for 10 minutes. The radar shows two drones operating at four miles up. I bet they are Reapers. And they are still a ways off but they are searching with lock-on codes."

"Meaning what," said Castillo.

"Meaning we are now a target. We've got to get out now."

"But what will happen to the Cuban?" said Castillo.

Everyone looked over at Omar. He was still dazed. He had several gunshot wounds in his torso. Merc was direct. "We'll bring him with us. It'll be messy but if he survives, I hope the Mexicans put him in jail for a long time. He's killed a lot of people from other cartels. Prison will not be a pleasant place for him."

By this time, Omar had regained consciousness. He had been listening. "Actually, I have never killed anyone. But you gringos did...including Francisco Arcangel, the head of the Equipo 30 cartel. I'm a Mexican drug agent. I've been after him for years. I need the small notebook he carries. It has contacts to other cartels. Find it. It could be in his jacket. Or in that case I was carrying that when La Gringa captured me."

Merc looked to Fernando. "Is that true? Is Omar a good guy?"

"Well. I don't know about the book," said Fernando, "but I have heard of Omar. Yes, I think he is on our side."

Merc loosened the rope binding Omar's hands. Omar turned to Fernando. "Amigo. You've got to find that little notebook now. Where is his body?"

Fernando searched through Francisco's jacket. "No notebook."

"Then it's in his case. Where is the case? I had the case when that goat woman tied me up."

Merc looked over. "I brought the case back. It's around here somewhere."

Eliot was increasingly agitated. The piercing buzzer now beeped louder, more frenetically. "Gotta go. Gotta go. No time. No time. Get the hell out." He was wide-eyed and crazy, wild and screaming. Eliot started pushing people out of the cave. "Hear that. Hear that. The drones have found us. They can't see us because of the way the rocks flow, but they know electronically where we are. And we are close to a lock-on by a Hellfire missile. We don't have time. We have to get the fuck out now. This place will blow."

Merc and Enrique struggled to drag out the two dead gunmen. Shay and Ruby pulled Francisco's body roughly out the cave mouth and down the narrow trail. Eliot gathered his own notebooks and stuffed them in a backpack, than ran from the cave.

Omar continued to protest until Fernando half-carried him through the cave mouth. Fernando was last in the traffic jam on the trail. Omar pried himself loose from Fernando. "Keep running. I'm coming."

Fernando pushed ahead. For the last 50 yards, he helped drag the body of one dead gunman.

Eliot was screaming for everyone to move quickly. The jumbled procession finally managed to reach a bend in the canyon and move around it, out of sight of the cave mouth.

Eliot turned. "We'll be safe here. Everyone here?"

"Looks like it," said Merc. But Fernando scanned the

group. "The Cuban. He's not here."

Eliot looked around the corner but couldn't see anyone on the trail.

"Now we have to move fast. Shoot up some guns and get to the vehicles. The military will be here as soon as they can find this place."

Just then, the thrum of a drone echoed off the canyon's wall and a silver glint appeared in the sky over the arroyo. All eyes turned to el mosco. They could see the flashes as the missiles fired, screaming in toward H's workshop.

The Hellfires were deadly accurate. They delivered thunderous blasts, lighting up the arroyo and setting off a deafening trio of secondary explosions, each sending a mushroom of dust and debris into the sky. The rocks above the cave spilled down and the opening simply disappeared.

44

The Wall of Fame

 "Hooper, this place still is a dump."

"It is small, sir. Sometimes, we even double up in the cubicles." Agent Hooper was sitting at a corner desk, finishing notes on his day's patrol.

"I'll work on getting you guys additional office space." Captain Tank Dolan had forgotten how cramped the conditions were at the Border Protection's Yuma station. He had only been gone for two months, having been promoted to regional deputy district administrator after the Equipo 30 cartel had been dismantled. The Yuma office was a slum compared to his starkly modern office in the federal building overlooking Mission Bay in San Diego. Yuma seemed like the distant past.

But to Dolan, the most upsetting shock in the Yuma office was the colorful photo montage staring down from the Wall of Honor. There, next to the three presidential citations for Edgar Castillo and the giant color portrait of El Toro, was the newly posted glossy photograph of

Enrique Castillo with his arm raised to pat the fuselage of the drone Charley 2. Under the picture, was Castillo's new nickname, "El Aguila," the eagle.

Dolan was aghast. *How could this happen? The biggest fuckup in the Yuma office is now sharing a Wall of Honor spot with the greatest, hardest working agent of all time, his father.*

Dolan had come back to Yuma today to preside over the rare Presidential citation ceremony. The honoree, of course, was Pilot Agent Enrique Castillo, the newly promoted air interdiction supervisor for the Yuma district.

Castillo was to be recognized for spearheading the discovery of the fugitive leader of the Equipo 30 drug cartel, breaking up their anti-drone activities and working with a retired Mexican drug agent to find the missing Predator drone that had been spoofed from the sky. The ceremony would be in the drone's hangar at the Yuma Marine Corps Air Station headquarters, where he also would also have to drape a medal on the nose of the newly rebuilt drone Charley 2 and honor its support staff. They were getting Presidential Notices for their contributions to the operation.

A government car was waiting to take the celebrities to the hangar. Captain Dolan rode with Castillo and the geeky Ellen Byrne. She was the reedy scientist with tousled hair, pronounced overbite and large clear-rimmed glasses that had headed the liaison with FlyTomics during the Equipo 30 cartel assaults. She now designed anti-drone systems for the U.S. Air Force through a Department of Defense contract.

"Miss Byrne. Congratulations. I heard you and Agent Castillo will be married soon."

"Thank you, sir," Ellen said. "It'll be in December. We are hoping you will be able to come. QuiQue talks all the time about you."

"Yes, I would very much like to be there. Only a very important operation could keep me away." *Actually, anything could keep me away,* he thought.

Dolan glanced over at Agent Enrique Castillo, dressed in an elegant suit. Here was an agent who disobeyed orders, went off on his own, brought widely publicized shame to the Yuma office, almost destroyed Dolan's career and who was just shy of being headed to internal disciplinary hearings on morals violations; now, he would be getting the Customs and Border Protection Service's highest honor.

Captain Dolan was well aware that things could have gone the other way. He would love someday to hear the real story of what happened that day in the canyon west of Playa Refugio. When the government choppers finally reached the site 45 minutes after the missiles fired, they found the two agents and three dead cartel members in a riverbed clearing. Border Protection investigators believed they had evidence that there might have been five or six people involved in the firefight, not just Fernando and Enrique, and that there had been six or seven different weapons fired. They also found evidence that someone set off plastic explosives further up the canyon wall in the cave struck by the Hellfire missiles. But none of the witnesses had lived. The cave was sealed. The Cuban, whom

Dolan had learned was an agent for the federales anti-narco squad, must have died in the cave. They decided to skip any further investigation.

Pilot Agent Enrique Castillo's life was back on track. Now the supervising drone officer in the Yuma office, he also headed joint aerial surveillance with the Mexican government. The squads had been very successful lately, and the Mexicans had opened up more territory to cover.

More importantly was his joy at his rejuvenated domestic situation. His family was pleased with his fiancé, the very brainy scientist. Her influence had made a remarkable change in Enrique's outlook.

The couple bought a house in Yuma. He and Ellen decorated it with large glossy pictures of experimental drones, and of the miniature Skyfire air-to-air missiles she had designed, missiles now routinely carried on drones to protect against attacks. These weapons were the current game changers, and she was developing better ones on her new job with the Air Force.

The evenings at the new Byrne-Castillo house were the most exhilarating. Each day, Enrique couldn't wait to tell Ellen about the exciting drone patrols, and about how his pilots flew the drones with great precision using her new air combat tactics and drone-to-drone missiles.

Ellen listened raptly to his stories, and then would excuse herself to prepare a vegetable stew in the kitchen, where she pursued her hobby of gourmet, healthy meals. Finally, after a glass or two of wine, they would slip out of their clothes and run around the house naked, carrying model drones and chasing each other, making motor noises and re-enacting the most exciting drone busts of the day. After that, of course, when they were exhausted, they would fall into each other's arms and there would be rapture, something Pilot Agent Enrique Castillo now had time to savor.